*On the Margins of Great Empires*

Also by Andrew Duncan

Poetry

*In a German Hotel*
*Cut Memories and False Commands*
*Sound Surface*
*Alien Skies*
*Switching and Main Exchange* *
*Pauper Estate* *
*Anxiety Before Entering a Room. New and selected poems*
*Surveillance and Compliance*
*Skeleton Looking at Chinese Pictures*
*The Imaginary in Geometry*
*Savage Survivals (amid modern suavity)* *
*Threads of Iron* *
*In Five Eyes* *
*Radio Vortex* (ed. Norbert Lange — translated into German)

Criticism

*The Poetry Scene in the Nineties* (internet only)
*Centre and Periphery in Modern British Poetry* **
*The Failure of Conservatism in Modern British Poetry* **
*Origins of the Underground*
*The Council of Heresy* *
*The Long 1950s* *
*A Poetry Boom 1990-2010* *
*Fulfilling the Silent Rules* *


As editor

*Don't Start Me Talking* (with Tim Allen)
Joseph Macleod: *Cyclic Serial Zeniths from the Flux*
Joseph Macleod: *A Drinan Trilogy: The Cove / The Men of the Rocks / Script from Norway* (co-edited with James Fountain)

* original Shearsman titles
** revised second editions from Shearsman

# Andrew Duncan

# On the Margins of Great Empires

—Selected Poems—

Shearsman Books

First published in the United Kingdom in 2018 by
Shearsman Books
50 Westons Hill Drive
Emersons Green
BRISTOL
BS16 7DF

Shearsman Books Ltd Registered Office
30–31 St. James Place, Mangotsfield, Bristol BS16 9JB
*(this address not for correspondence)*

www.shearsman.com

ISBN 978-1-84861-598-4

Copyright © Andrew Duncan, 2018.

The right of Andrew Duncan to be identified as the author
of this work has been asserted by him in accordance with the
Copyrights, Designs and Patents Act of 1988.
All rights reserved.

### Acknowledgements

Some of these poems have been published in a number of magazines, from 1978 on. My thanks to all the editors who ever used the Yes word, especially to Ralph Hawkins, Rod Mengham, John Wilkinson, and Tim Longville (of *Ochre*, *Equofinality* and *Grosseteste Review*, respectively) who took my work on when I was off the map.

My thanks to Karlien van den Beukel for literary advice and counsel.

### Cover

*Portrait of Captain Joseph Huddart*, by Guan Zuolin of Macao, painted ca. 1785.
Oil on glass (reverse painted), 84.5 x 66.5 cms. Private Collection.

# Contents

Foreword                                                              7

### from *Threads of Iron* (1980-81)

Turkish Music                                                        11
In Charnwood                                                         17
A blue contract of employment,
    filled in as "Manpower Engineer"             19
Dead wind                                                            21
Dhofar                                                               23
"Laughing man"                                                       25
Almond Wind                                                          27

### from *Skeleton Looking at Chinese Pictures* (1983-87)

Nomad Carpets                                                        30
Griffin Carved in Walrus Ivory                                       33
Light                                                                34
About Living Opposite the Brewery in Brick Lane                      37
The June Sun Cast as the Absent Lover                                40
Shapeshifting and mismatches                                         42

### from *Alien Skies* (1993)

The Fallen Stone Tells the Poet How to Write                         44
In High Places                                                       46

### from *Sound Surface* (1992)

Jadis j'ai cru                                                       48
Circular                                                             51

### from *Surveillance and Compliance* (1987-92)

Roots of a Revolution                                                52
The Policy of Weakness                                               56
Heat Loss                                                            59

At Camden Lock 61
Tuyau as heat lens 63
Shiny Circuitry 65
Fragments of the Above 67

## Uncollected (1991-6)

At Cumae 69
Three Graves 71
For C. 75
Wind and Wear at Aix-en-Provence 80
Triumph and Martyrdom of Sergei Korolev 83

## from *Pauper Estate* (1996-9)

Looks like luxury and feels like a disease 86
Adesso non posso 89
Least Energy Structures 93
Snow-Puffed Plumage 95
The Technique of Visualising 96

## from *Savage Survivals* (1999-2005)

Precipice of Niches 98
Andy-the-German Servant of Two Masters 102
From Zenith to Pupil 106
Weapons Form with Music, #18 107

## from *The Imaginary in Geometry* (1999-2003)

The Ruins of Guldursun 108
The Spirit Mover, 1854 110
Q-landscapes 112
On the Beach at Aberystwyth 116
Abundance 121
When Myth Becomes History 123
Silver Threads and Golden Needles 126
Trust 128
Les Paul's Garage Studio 130

# Foreword

Age 23, age 50. You can't be the same person over 30 years. The voice is at first young and excitable, later on serene and even slothful. The poems don't converge on a focal point, and if there was a method, it was volatility and volubility. The poems come in groups and remain stranded in time. Frames close and open. If you weren't young and ignorant you wouldn't carry out this unrestrained behaviour whose disasters will bring you the embodied knowledge which will enable you to avoid falling off things, including verse forms, when you are older. Yes, yes, yes. Tell me to shut up. My father was a historian of astronomy and my mother taught German to engineers, both at Loughborough. Anywhere near a technological university in the Sixties, a golden horizon beckoned. 1974, leave school and work for a year as a labourer in England and Germany. I did metalworking (for a few months). 1975, study at Cambridge, mainly Anglo-Saxon, Norse and Celtic. It was the barbarian Tripos. Read 8th century sagas, write orderly prose essays in response, want to write Gaelic sagas in response. Was that boundary the pivot of everything? the frame in which perception is held steady, or paralysed? When it came to Anglo-Saxon work made of metal, somatic and abstract memory interfused—this really turned me on. They called it a forgery but it was an anvil.

In 1977-8 I wrote *In a German Hotel*, about being a guest worker, in a punk style approximating to pidgin German, as in a basically Turkish workplace. My voice started up, it wasn't my voice. *Ochre* magazine published this in 1978. After three years of punk I wanted to hear something softer and more expansive. This wasn't exactly an original idea. "The infinite compression of punk breaks up into a boundless release, the rediscovery of melody and colour," I wrote. 1978, move to London and suffer from homesickness. From 1978 to 1987 I was working at the New Southgate works of Standard Telephone and Cable. In 1980-1 I wrote *Threads of Iron*, "attempting [...] documentary poetry about the situation at work, where the basic power relations never slip out of mind: an unending cascade of concrete and puzzling problems, of human conjunctures. The real ordinance of society follows an ideology which is secret, covered by a false public one." J.H. Prynne liked this one a lot and it came out in two parts after a brief delay (*Cut Memories and False Commands* in 1991 and *Switching and Main Exchange* in 2001; the complete manuscript appeared in one volume, finally, from Shearsman in 2013). I didn't get published in the 1980s. In 1983-87 I wrote *Skeleton Looking at Chinese Pictures*, which was my concerted attempt to be a mainstream poet. Peter Porter liked it a lot but it only came out in 2000. *Surveillance and Compliance* was written between 1987 and 1992 and published in 2004 (it wasn't really finished until then). The firm I worked for hit big trouble in 1986 and shed about 20,000 jobs in two years. *Surveillance and Compliance* was an attempt to write about this from the workforce's point of view. Whatever you write about, people will try to ascribe it to your personality. It is also about Squatland and people whose personalities overwhelmed them so much they simply couldn't do anything else. 'Nimble and competitive', I wrote. Compliance and Surveillance were two IT projects I worked on at a City regulatory body.

At the end of the Eighties, I discovered the poetic Underground. Close up, they weren't invisible. I got involved with other poets of my own age. I wondered why they didn't write like me. Never found out. In 1991, I got a book out. In 1992 I wrote *Sound Surface*, which was a follow-up to *Threads* and came out in 1993. In 1993, I wrote *Alien Skies*, published 1993. This was a detached project about rockets and meteorites. *Pauper Estate* is about being on the dole and repeats useful government advice on how to keep warm when you can't afford to turn the heating on. The cold is offset by the smoke of besetting and nostalgic hallucinations not only about an ex-lover but also about industrial activity. It came out in 2000, I had a job by then. *The Imaginary in Geometry* and *Savage Survivals (amid modern suavity)* were written slowly from 1999 and came out in 2005 and 2006. Some of the poems included come from 'Anglophilia, a romance of the docks', a series about staging, or editing, national myth. 'Q-landscapes' is about advertising as "capitalist realism". *Radio Vortex* was my selected poems translated into German and came out in 2017.

"On the margins of great empires" refers to the poem 'When Myth Becomes History' and to folk culture as a buried horizon. I wrote "in *Threads* [...] some of what appears to be folksong is me. Wealth and impoverishment; two strands."

Andrew Duncan

*To Norbert Lange and Ulf Stolterfoht*

# Turkish Music

Lightly holding the purple reins
We leap to the saddle, our tasselled helmets low,
Our banners fluttering like crimson clouds,
Writhing like snakes and dragons in the air.
Deploying in nine rings we laugh to scorn
This petty Empire. Can the Hans withstand
The mighty Tartars?
As we display our might, the roar of the drums
Strikes fear into all who hear;
The bugles sound to form the ranks for battle.
   —Hong Sheng, *The Palace of Eternal Youth* (1688), scene 16


Midnight has settled on the village square outside,
Where the cattle drive twice a day.
Under my room, in the peasants' house of wood and plaster
Used by the hotel workers
Is the room where the work permit men live out five years,
No family allowed and no respite from the Germans,
To return to Anatolia with the capital.
Time lost, knowledge of death;
Memory lost, narrow and bitter as a knife;
Hearts lost, a gamble of despair
With happiness.
I think of my home but see nothing definite.
I remember the day. Darkness pours in from the snowy forest
And there music is falling from the air.

"At home, the landowners form all sides in parliament,
Control each policy, each wing of the truth.
The man without money is like a wisp of the air
Dressed in old clothes and a skin chapped with too many nerves,
Trying to move against the great wind
Which moans
The breadth of the high steppes.
The poor man trying to move forward out of nothing
Is like the Yuruk, the nomad shepherd blown march by march

Destroying the grass and fleeing
Before a force he cannot name.
Where is he going? he has no rest but his longing,
No earth but his song.
Land is like the taint of race darkening the blood,
Possession is like the rocks: unchangeable.
Peasants are like animals, they cannot own.

We'll irrigate the desert.
We'll give the land to the tiller.

Once the conquerors, horse nomads,
Dealt out the land and broken peoples
To Counts maintaining soldiers, sipahis—
The Army created the State, and the nation was a honeycomb of warriors.
We sowed wheat, harvested ranks of men.
We who were owned, owned nothing.
Nomads, with flocks of men… Today we own nothing
And the rich are not bound to service…

When will I own the farm I served with hand and eye?
When I leave this country
(I have never learnt German)
I will buy a flock of white sheep
I will buy a flock of black sheep
I will buy a grove of lemon trees.
I will raise tomatoes, on that ground more fertile than any other.
I will raise a family to work it.
We will grow enough to eat.
I will buy a share of land, as much as I can till.
No more hunger. But then, the distributors, the buyers…"

They drink and laugh late into the German morning.
We start work at 7:30.
They play electric Turkish music.
It is like the furls
Of molten bronze poured into a cauldron of milk.
It is as if the ashes of night

Shone through with the red grate of stellar fire.
As if the Scorpion, fiery, pinned to the apse of sky,
Arched.
It was like the spasm of my most contorted and strong nerves.
It was like understanding the language of birds.
It was like the taste of copper earth, acrid and binding for ever.
It was the spice of air.
I want to sleep. Instead I listen to this music.
It is as if the waterways of ore within the earth
Belled.

My breath, gasp and heart's heart, is outside me.
I riffle an unskeined pack of memories, heartless shadows.
I have no dwelling in this earth, no possession.
The fields are lonely because they are not English.
I pine for those sensations.
Can you tell me where my country lies?

Does the wind
Turn the dust into birds?
Such are embers of a total song
For whom the earth is nothing but what passes
Hidden in a shriek of wind and blood,
Of passage and ardour.
Song, flown from a far country,
Masonry of the invisible cities,
Architecture of the streets of longing,
Where the singing of women is heard behind barred, fretted windows.
It may be the songs of lovers,
Gay goshawks fluttering against those lattices;
Or the wailing for dead husbands, archaic—
The voice of stone shattering—
Stomach knotted with aloes, resin of sharpness, tight throat;
*Agit*, barb of frenzy.

Because I know you will never understand my song
Because I know I will never understand this music
Because when you sing, at work,
The heedless song is alien in your throats; because my thoughts are lost in
The distance towards home;

I know beauty is not a form, but affection, a memory
Of your mother, or breath purified in a kiss.
The face in my heart is hard for me to see.
Once we danced and sang in front of men,
Shouting aloud the words we hear when alone.
Exhaustion beat the devils and motion fired our cold clay.
Running in shapes, we left everything behind
And sang in the metre of the triple leap:
triumpe, triumpe, triumpe...
Our dancing days are done. And you drink to forget everything:

"In the Altai mountains,
In Turkestan, in the time of the making of nations
When men were hardly different from soil
The first Turk lived with his sheep and mares.
Our people lived in a valley of brass ringed by an iron mountain.
There was no path through the dark rock
Till we were led to freedom by a grey wolf,
Into the world by a hidden path.
The great steppes were lit by a Sun of blazing iron,
Rare grasses led us over beckoning plains...

Led by a wolf to the slums of the city
We blow through German streets
Like scraps of newspaper
Absorbing dirt
Always empty.

Protect us, great dervish.
We are so many, none can count us
We are so many, none can defeat us
We are so few, no enemy can find us.
We are so many, none can feed us.
We must go to foreigners to ask for rule.
We are sons of the Sun and the whole earth is ours.
We take orders from those who take orders.

Give us
The song in the language in which our names are pure and no longer insults,

The air with the Arabian or Balkan flourishes
Like the song used to melt the pain of surgery
In the mountains of the east, where there are few doctors.
There the men sing more strongly than the knife
The song of opium, chant like a second heart
That lets the mind float free in its strength.
Be with us, great dervish. We are so many
None is lonely. None is proud.

We were conquerors, we were slaves.
Will we rise one day when this world ends
Across the bridge of fire and the labouring day
To the space distilling like resin from a slashed tree,
Where the walls of each soul give way
And we are one?"

Up here, I have no music. The melody eludes the tongue.
The lone Puritan voice in the white room
Moves upward from the realm of passions.
We have advanced by severance, deriving thought from loneliness.
The neoterics
Search out archaic words and the unreal past;
And ritualists teach rosaries not knowing what they mean.
Since we have no common and musical speech
Language is reduced to tags of class.
In each image they see a room
And in each room a social rank.

This is a room for kitchen workers to sleep in,
But what we feel is free and up to us.
In the raw night the black storm of music—
You'd think the house poured brandy down a throat of garlic—
Plucks my nerves although my limbs are still.
Pictures run in my head and I am the pictures.
I love this electric music,
Its violence is like the writhe of struggling men, working men.

Each new form is made in the dark
And the old one is like soil buried beneath the earth.
As the millennia of tradition become a basic silence;

*In Germany*

When the ornamentation has borne itself down,
And worked itself into a flower with no stem;
When the unspent day is a cruelly stylized space;
I'll remember
Turkish music.

"The drinkers of fermented mares' milk;
The pagans who anointed their Banners with milk in triumph;
The smokers of opium, chasing the heavy fumes
Like the red heart of a black night;
Drink in this landscape of man,
These woods-and-fields of man,
And are pined.

I would like to sit beside the Aegean
Watching the fishing boats drift home at dusk.
I would pour water into the raki,
Which turns cloudy, the colour of lion's milk.
I would eat a lemon, to give it sharpness;
I would eat roast beef, to give it weight.
My family would be there beside me.
I would lack for nothing."

# In Charnwood

Three kinds of smooth: floods of the Soar, silver sheets of miles,
Black cleaves of rock, chafed and faced by forceful rain;
Slick clay, wet and split by a fork, or smooth inside itself.

Three kinds of red:
Red of hawthorn hedge, like a haze on the meshed twigs;
Red of the outcrop of rock at Mountsorrel;
Red light in the afternoon on walls, faces, clouds.

Three names of the province;
Coritani, worshippers of the Goddess Trent;
Raisers of the earthworks at Caer Lyr.
Mercia, the March: the military frontier. Landless mercenaries
Gnawed the Combroges to the bone of garrisoned Snowdonia.
Charnwood: burnt forest. Before America, this Great Wood
Or Hercynian darkness of wolves and mistletoe
Fed the seaward colonists.
Ash-keels tilled the North Sea, swan's way;
Fire drowned the stands of oak and beech.
Ash as rich as coin and fine as silk
Mulched the won fields.
In February, the burning;
In August, the reaping.

Three kinds of yellow:
Yellow of corn in July, Iraqi reed turned to fruit;
Yellow of hair, blond Danelaw strain, fair in the five boroughs,
Nordic light pointing-up the Indic raven on the street;
Yellow foam-flecks under the granite step of a waterfall.

Three kinds of curve:
The boar-back ridge, still untilled, lunges frozen;
The River Idle, winding through reed-beds, slow in the flat;
Pap dribbling down the bib of the earth.
Volutes of Coritanian metalwork,
Bedded back in the earth as if in the foundry sand once more.

*Threads of Iron* (1980-81)

Three kinds of shelter:
Rabbits in the delved conery, litters tippet each other,
Grass at the door like milk;
Earwigs in the apple's eye, the Riviera of wintering grubs;
And me sleeping in the town amongst my family.

Three more kinds of red:
The fox, sharp-set and brainy, roaming for his living;
Iron case-hardened in an open forge, in the small ironmaster's,
Like skin it changes on warming;
The coke shimmers and swims, neither gravel- nor starling-tint;
Stubble burning off in September, red and black in stripes
Like the furrows of happiness and sadness.

Three kinds of path:
Way of the bird in the air.
Folded winds are pillows of velocity.
He scoops up a song on a hook. One dipped wing
Will tip the world on its edge.
Gallery of the miner in the earth; lead and coal
Strap the stone of thick darkness
Like muscles rigid in some scouring task.
That is a path
Which the eye of the kestrel has not discovered
Nor the foot of the sons of pride.
The eater of the darkness to its rim
Has overturned mountains from the root.
Third
Thought's path in the mapped temples
Fissured like Switzerland.

# A blue contract of employment, filled in as "Manpower Engineer"; November, 1978

They ship you in from the hinterland
To the capital city. Bodies alongside the trucks
Full of setts & aggregate, migrating
From a region of hills whose streams drove wheels.
They reared the desert up on end and called it a City.

Memory and family and
Being loved and
Self love and
Spatial knowledge and
The body fitting into the landscape
Cease. The inside of your mind is torn out.
Refitted over years.

The air dying around my fingertips
The skin inside my body withering
My ideas falsified
By the volumes adjacent to me.
After storing all the things I hate,
Sensation has stopped.
Objects vanish in the gap.

Laying out the worksheets and totting.

Nimble fingers & bent back & quick to it
& go where the work is. If
You want what they've got
You'd better do what they say.

My body parts
To admit the dream.
Swill in the concept of Home
& close your eyes & drench in it
And make a symbol into your food. You evanesce.
The towns of childhood crumble into dust.

*Threads of Iron* (1980-81)

A tongue tralalas tired figures of consolation.

An ideal of myself
Spilt from its bag somewhere in the marshalling yard
Trodden in by the new batch of migrants
And blown with the wrapping papers.

Emotion is
The possession of the dispossessed &
The reasoning of the weak &
That food which makes you thin.

The job offer written on blue paper.
I fulfil the words of command
Listening to a severed voice of culture.

# Dead Wind

Storm winds scour the streets of the winter town.
Rags stir in an alley,
Eddies of grit blow in my eyes.
A scree of dust blows up the neck of the streets
Like shale down an empty stream bed.
Rubbish is thrown up on waste lots,
Bright colours of dead manufactures.
Odours wash from dumps and incinerators:
The pyres of carcasses which part flesh and bone.

Poor youths shelter between close walls,
Like sheep in a hollow on the moor.
They live out on the street and beg; high above
I stare out into the wind zone,
Flesh numbed in the flagrance of the idiot wind,
In the immunity. I listen to music.
My destiny written on torn scraps of paper
Goes round and round in the street, numb terrain.
A wind blows from the dead heart of things.
A vain liquid pulses in the canals of my ear,
Dead wind.

The streets are full of lies and fears and powers.
Intimate poses smile from posters, the frozen
Flesh blown up covers the side of buildings,
The drilling of images wearies the eye.
No-one looks at each other: broken gazes broken words.
Our assent creates huge chaussées,
Scoured by inhuman forces.
The cars crawl by like a reel of film in coma,
Grit roar and fumes waft up on a metal wind.
Commerce corrupts dead sense. The air is soaked in words…
Shapes in my mind buckle and taint, realigned
By null forces.
A sick wind creases the sky
A sick wind jars the words in my mouth.

*Threads of Iron* (1980-81)

Numbers, numbers
The tangent to the curve of change veers over,
The body of oppression bursts, its parts shift shape.
The axis starts to spin
The pure light falls on the pure lens
Material factors reverse their moments
The axis drives
The cup of bitterness is broken, the winged seeds
Plunge into the bridal earth. All movements
Find their end. How many more years?

Stone is winnowed on the threshing-floor of winds.
Vague cries from the death of matter.
The supple riddle sifts a grain of stone.
Tall buildings are ruined incessantly;
The edifice of thought shivers instantly.
Time swathes cities like a man walking through reeds.
A celestial jaw polishes the brick-husks into dust.
Verticality is laid low,
The hedges of struts cannot resist. The term
Of their arcs is ruin. Ruins of Time
Are the fauna of memory: living stones.
Stone reared up is the properties of the City,
Stone crumbled is the flesh of the black earth.
The living eye has read the scriptures to the end.

Your voice is torn away.
I see mouths rent open without a sound
I cannot catch the words.
A rat riddles the walls and substructures
A jackal slinks
Along the lines of towering graves.
Through broken windows and into deserted rooms
An oracle wind gasps out, in the dry skull of the City,
"How many more years?"
A dead wind drains the warmth from my head.
A sick wind drains the words in my mouth.

# Dhofar

The land got up and was gone,
Strode, rivers flashing and flowing, worms darting like nerve-ends.
This morning we are ten, now we are three.
Last year we were a hundred, now we are a hundred thousand.

We are the guerrillas.
Compared to us, rocks are seen to move
And lightning is slow.
We are the herb which tempts very rare animals to pasture
So that we can turn ourselves into them.
We turn black into green, and dart upwards
But we would prefer to hide beneath the soil!

We speak an idiom that is not Arabic
An idiom of the oppressed, of the mountains, of the gravel seas,
Of the oryx and kestrel.
It is the language of the illiterate,
A language to resist interrogators.
It is a language surpassing all others in beauty
For it acknowledges no rich and poor!
It is a speech like the air, good to breathe.
It is a buckle of brain sense and group action.

Here the rich man has no trachoma or TB, and speaks Arabic.
As for rich, he isn't so much;
Here is no oil, but still foreigners—
Bombardments from the sea. We never saw so much metal.
We have been ruled by slaves, we are in our rising.
We have no history but horses and incense.
Islam never won here. And now socialism.
We learn to read, to conquer the past and the sources of the future.
The British are broken, the Iranians have fled
The Sultan is a louse in the hair of slaves.

The pastor leads the cow from the byre covered with live grass,
Then he kneels under the irriguous belly and blows, blows,

So that the yielder knows to let the milk down.
Till twenty years ago, we did not know the sea disguised another nation,
We thought we were alone.
Foreigners blew in from the sea like the rare stones from the sky.
This is Ophir, Arabia Felix. Stones with diseased marrows have burnt the byre.
After the flail of blindness and the hook of wasting sickness
Here are the mortars, the helicopters, the offshore batteries.

Like the nerve conjoining the quilt of sinew to the shaft of bone
We pierce with information and electricity.
The army taught me how to read and since that time
Thought is different: it has more of myself.
Like worms we'll tread and slough
The ashen, choking sand into a grove of oranges,
We'll drown the fine lady, the pomegranate,
Whose fruit young girls sew onto their robe next to bells,
Into the crumb of the soil.

You occupy the territory, we are it.
We stoop like night hawks in the black fear of our enemies.
We have compassed their foreheads with steel bands,
We have bowed our heads and cut their sinews behind the knee.
One was despair, two was comprehension, three was victory.
Four was the head flush with the stones of the choked watercourse.

Three nations invaded us: Iran, Britain, Saudi Arabia.
On the sea, America. Count only
A hundred and fifty thousand
And you have passed beyond our tongue
And added strangers to our nation.
We will outlast.
We menace like a limestone land sieved by corrosive water.
They will vanish into the generosity of our glorious past.
We will bear them, bier them to their graves.
We will break their metals like threads.
Rocks surge from the earth to bury them.
We are the earth in motion. We are the javelins of the sun.

*Threads of Iron* (1980-81)

## "Laughing Man": self-portrait by Richard Gerstl

The laugh is a black pulse out, blackout,
It smells the heretic's pyre.

The air is flayed,
It gashes in a livid, greenish, throttle.
Membranes are choked with a gulp of combusting gas.
His face is a red devil-mask of wood the peasants wear
(Draped and masked we go down the mountainside towards the village
Bounding and leaping)
His rictus gasps in the world like a white flame of Alpine air.

Artistic forms burn up in a cyclonic opiate rush
Nerves pour back from the head to the entrails, the crawlers
The self-portrait is a skin above a mask
Consumptive slum-girls strike the noble classical poses
The marble effigies in the royal staterooms
Cover each other in red booths as small as ovens

He laughs at the years of labour like coma
Real experience slips through the blocks of habit like a thief
Work? what was that?
Instinct is an old dog and intelligence is lethal.
He laughs
Like a man throwing up the intoxication of life
And passing out.
"I am God, I made this caricature."

Laughing, the eyes of buildings go black—
Diaphragms taut, bellowing, ripped—
The images in their windows crack,
Their bones are carious.

The lizards in the formal gardens are marked with laughing heads.
The dressed stone turns to the soft animal beneath it.

When such a man laughs

*Threads of Iron* (1980-81)

Paper shares are worth no more than what a painter scrawls on
Brokers drink themselves into a coma
Money grows sick and whirls like fever dreams
The Palace of Justice burns, and the book of land deeds with it
The expression of the double eagles
Unfurled to fly through Serbia or the Kirghiz Steppe
Twists until it is his.

# Almond Wind: Lament for Osip Mandelshtam

A wind blew in the region of the Black Sea.
It was like the outcry of a bird.
It carried enough almond blossom
To hide the surface of a lake.
It blew
A note so pure it drank the enthralled air
And drifted on the European shore.
Where it ruffled
A face formed on the water.

The rain-bearing wind cast down a lake.
The lake has a triple form:
The choppy lake turned to a fish's cold and broken skin;
The lake given by the night an endless starry depth;
The lake firm and bright as glass
Which frees the eye and accedes to the total blue.
As in the stressed languages the steps of ictus—
Pinions, spirit hammer, quivers along the cord of air—
Ascend from height to height of lifting breath
In the tiers of stress, so
The superlative draws the mind;
As a slope draws water across the broken horizons of earth,
Through the pitches of matter.
The lake forms the image of an almond tree.

A word was spoken
In that stellar black;
A rhythm crossed the inner span of darkness.
Matter shook itself like dust on a cymbal,
Mountains froze along the globe's chords,
And a green wind raised trees from clay and light.
Then, rocks and trees moved at man's command,
And all sang to meet the rising sun.

When the Thracians tore him limb from limb
The sun died with the eye of Orpheus,

*Threads of Iron* (1980-81)

Space turned to division as his motion ceases,
The sap of the flowers perished with his fluids
And measure was parted by his dismembered language.
A generation of spectres caught up his phrase.
The poisonous yew ate up the white and fluttering birch,
And the birch sleeps frozen in the cask of yew.
Drilled masses shook the earth, marching to song,
The ash-shafts struck roots and estates in the slatted sky:
Spear-leaves, a forest of hammered sun, shimmered.
Scythians paused on the mountain hinge between sea and sea,
Cast wooden lots upon a painted drum,
And moved out onto the plain to found States.

Now, snow takes up the tongues of rivers, pierces the fruit's flesh:
And the snow takes up the buried shapes like Reason.
Thralls work the seigneurial furrows,
And a warrior caste reaps and winnows peoples.
When he unleashed the screams we still hear
The true sound of trees and waters died
And the sun was darkened by corrupted sight.
Madness slurslurs the rhythm of words to bestiality,
And the work-gang's drum beats without grace or tremor.
The mountain man stands in the middle of Saint Petersburg,
And the sycophant rhymes slaughterhouse with altar.

Where the wind ruffles the pool
A face forms in the water. I mimic it,
Worship it, disperse it, ask it questions.
How should I arrange my days? my thoughts?
Thoughts die as they flow, to leave,
Each one, a part of the measure; the safety of the plant
Is in the rhythm: how seeds pulse to recur and seed,
What men cut into glass or write on linen;
Or what strophes the wind recites.
Because what's said can never be silenced
We part from each word to replete the measure.
Oh, voice inside,
The stream bearing images between light and the dark fastness,
Which scales, shoots, sprays; is steeped and tinged and
Driven by great swept-axis blades;

*Threads of Iron* (1980-81)

# Almond Wind: Lament for Osip Mandelshtam

A wind blew in the region of the Black Sea.
It was like the outcry of a bird.
It carried enough almond blossom
To hide the surface of a lake.
It blew
A note so pure it drank the enthralled air
And drifted on the European shore.
Where it ruffled
A face formed on the water.

The rain-bearing wind cast down a lake.
The lake has a triple form:
The choppy lake turned to a fish's cold and broken skin;
The lake given by the night an endless starry depth;
The lake firm and bright as glass
Which frees the eye and accedes to the total blue.
As in the stressed languages the steps of ictus—
Pinions, spirit hammer, quivers along the cord of air—
Ascend from height to height of lifting breath
In the tiers of stress, so
The superlative draws the mind;
As a slope draws water across the broken horizons of earth,
Through the pitches of matter.
The lake forms the image of an almond tree.

A word was spoken
In that stellar black;
A rhythm crossed the inner span of darkness.
Matter shook itself like dust on a cymbal,
Mountains froze along the globe's chords,
And a green wind raised trees from clay and light.
Then, rocks and trees moved at man's command,
And all sang to meet the rising sun.

When the Thracians tore him limb from limb
The sun died with the eye of Orpheus,

Space turned to division as his motion ceases,
The sap of the flowers perished with his fluids
And measure was parted by his dismembered language.
A generation of spectres caught up his phrase.
The poisonous yew ate up the white and fluttering birch,
And the birch sleeps frozen in the cask of yew.
Drilled masses shook the earth, marching to song,
The ash-shafts struck roots and estates in the slatted sky:
Spear-leaves, a forest of hammered sun, shimmered.
Scythians paused on the mountain hinge between sea and sea,
Cast wooden lots upon a painted drum,
And moved out onto the plain to found States.

Now, snow takes up the tongues of rivers, pierces the fruit's flesh:
And the snow takes up the buried shapes like Reason.
Thralls work the seigneurial furrows,
And a warrior caste reaps and winnows peoples.
When he unleashed the screams we still hear
The true sound of trees and waters died
And the sun was darkened by corrupted sight.
Madness slurslurs the rhythm of words to bestiality,
And the work-gang's drum beats without grace or tremor.
The mountain man stands in the middle of Saint Petersburg,
And the sycophant rhymes slaughterhouse with altar.

Where the wind ruffles the pool
A face forms in the water. I mimic it,
Worship it, disperse it, ask it questions.
How should I arrange my days? my thoughts?
Thoughts die as they flow, to leave,
Each one, a part of the measure; the safety of the plant
Is in the rhythm: how seeds pulse to recur and seed,
What men cut into glass or write on linen;
Or what strophes the wind recites.
Because what's said can never be silenced
We part from each word to replete the measure.
Oh, voice inside,
The stream bearing images between light and the dark fastness,
Which scales, shoots, sprays; is steeped and tinged and
Driven by great swept-axis blades;

You are the little breath, all
That father and mother bequeath us.
What days come to us
When that voice is once untuned?
Their air carries us to a far land.
Unskimmed by angels, we still hear
It beating around our heads. By lakes at sunrise;
As agonists in love; in
Discussions by night;
We glimpse the true and sheafing Spring, the green wind.

A pure wind wafts the white flurries;
Its scansion is higher than the rigorous stave.
Snow falls on your bare head as you turn away,
An old Jew thinly dressed among the work-gang.
A wind blew over the shores of the Black Sea.

## Nomad Carpets

The women weave it where they rest of the evenings,
An hour for each square inch, knotting each tuft under the mat;
A circuit of the year for each completed carpet—
Until the shuttle of the year has shot
From beam to beam of the draped frame of heaven,
From door to door of the Sophia of suspended sky.
The emptiness
Stretches out towards the scant moisture of the eye.
The year
Is one long march. They weave...
Where the fodder is rich, they can rest.

The rovers of the infinite pasture sift the earth crumb by crumb,
Vast eyres trod out root by root—leaf by leaf—mouthful by mouthful.
The needle passes through the balks like a worm through sand.
The thread passes through the needle's eye
Like rootlets through soil.
The kindred walks through the migration loop
Like a river towards an Asian lake.

Great winds quarter the earth.
We hear the voice of the steppe and the depositor of loess:
Tatar wind
Aryan wind
Heavy and rich
Blows for thousands of years invariant, eddies of the Pole turning
Like the hub of the Year.

The gold-bearing wind, fleeced with wheat,
Flows like a river of air across the continent;
The black grain of the blue threshing-floor
Cascades onto the plains like flour, like ore.
The flaws of wind-silt sift and trickle
Onto the dark lands where the nomad ends:
Millet and villages and fieldmarks.

Over markless lands
The Polovtsian wind, a body of dust and husks
On a nag of air
Spells out the path of the militarized khanates.
Following the worn lines of their cosmologies,
The hordes move like giant gusts of air
From the rising sun to the falling;
From Ch'in's Great Wall to where the miles of abattis
Guard the Polesian Forest.

The nomad flickers
Like veins of smoke in the saltern between stars and flint.
He rushes like horses mad with heat
Over a steppe of wormwood and wolves' lairs and chariot-graves
Into the sunset gleaming like the flanks of a roan stallion;
Orbs rise and fall,
The silver cord hoists a dark blue canopy, the yurt of heaven.
The nap of drape-darkness is sleek as silk,
The Khan of stars folds in his flock with sleep.

In the tent is the richer darkness of the carpet,
Narrator of earth, wetlands: when drought kills off the old
And the flocks are too weak to find the next grazing,
(The Shepherd carries a tender lamb across his shoulders),
The carpet is a mass of lilies in a pond and
The flash of fish in a sluice.
It's said the coursers of aridity smell water on the wind:
Intensity of the whetted senses! perfection of the starved palate!

The carpets are woven by women dreaming,
"Bells and pomegranates fringe your robe,
Trees and stars adorn its breast.
I count the flecks of your eye, Sulamith:
They are like the bowers of the garden.
The embroidered tunic decks you in a garden,
Veiling the loved body in coolness.
You appear as tender pools and flowering trees;
You are fragrant as a grove of lemons in the waste."

Carpet of the shepherds out under the stars,
Narrator of the courses of the sky:
The vastness of the summer where a far haze and heaven's arch-tiles
Lash the endless eye, darting a plain without walls or fieldmarks,
And noon surges like the clangs of the bronze, flawless, bell;
Like the curved mouth of an angel singing.
At midnight
Stars roam a deep blue screen clear as mathematics
Along the coronets which span the brow of the sky,
Like weft threads drawing across a sable ground,
Like clasps along the enchasement of the stargems.

In the cloudy steppes
Ülgen and Erlik Khan fight for the sway of the nine worlds.

Narrator of the drift of reverie.
What I see in the carpet:
Lyres, vases, taut silk bridges, fronds,
Bines, pinions, bays, swoops, glassblown gasps,
Feathers and oases, islets, mare's tail clouds,
Swales, Kufic strophes, pierced screens, hanging gardens…

*Skeletons Looking at Chinese Pictures* (1983-1987)

# Griffin Carved in Walrus Ivory

Frozen splash
Held shear of knife
Flesh-riving spray
White tear
Fretted grinder of spine and salt sea spray.

In the dim ocean the walrus is a spark of heat,
Plunging in the darkness behind the sunset.
The toppling cliffs of water close above its eyes.
In the North and sun-fall of the Ocean,
The wanderer is dashed
Between the freezing finials of the World-Snake himself,
Where the white water chilled by his viscera swirls,
Issuing from the river of death and darkness.
The main pours through the freezing basins of the world
Like masses of chilled blood through a grieving heart.
You go to some Atlantic island to calve; Hesperides of gale and rock
Where, striving Spring seeds, you find the fertile air.

Kernel
Living stone concerted of blood and nerve
In your core-skull is carved the winged lion
Who clutches in Scythia with frozen claws
The crop of winter: gold,
Fruit of Decembers where light died of chill
To vein the Finnic tundra with scoriac sun-glacier.
There, Scyths work the gold on pommels and chariots,
The snow falling on their forges hisses rarely.

# Light

Metal bursts into flame
The daystar blows up, grinding
Iron into light.
The meridian ore booms as it folds,
Axes crackle across the gold orb.
Polarized by the waves in the ferric core.
The noon of blazing metal shakes
Percoursed by deep vibrations, shuddering out
Ionic winds, light torrents, and heavy sparks.

Rays retain the spectral gaps of metals.
All things are an exchange for fire,
And fire for all things; even as gold
For wares and wares for gold.
Flame sleeps under the sill of matter,
And the world is the ash of many burnings.
Light is the slag of sidereal metal,
Its visible freight is the ashes of things.
Form itself comes from the furnace of the sun,
And the potency of the smith is born in the forge.
I read the book of fire:
Cities on flame with noon light crumple up
Lakes drown in fire poured on by sunset
I saw the dancer, falling away from the earth
I saw the jealous man hollowed out and calcined
I saw the smith turning his body into force
I saw passion burn the wood of men
I saw the fire of Time eat up the nine-walled city

The fledged light, borne in stalks of fennel,
Tumbles to earth.
The shards of the blazing star
Annunciate
The forms of the fallen world.

The flames which are also signs
Tarnished with their message of clay, merged
Till Kingdom Come with husks of darkness
Lick at my head.
As if I stood under a tree bent with fruit, whose
Skins impaired by wasps splashed and dripped
Juice in ferment on my thirst:
So vineyards of light burst in brilliant smoke.

Fruits and eyes are splinters of the sun,
Dazed and residual on the shores of a falling river.
Dim eyes close on my winter depression,
Grow bright as the day fills out its flanks.
As berries soak in sunlight, by which
The dark parts inhume that
Taut and gorgeous swell of fruit: so
The eye soaks in object-light, a loving stream
Which laps and glides along my eye-apple.
In that rich smoke of things visible
The eye swells to currant lushness;
In the soft trace of stars and trees and men
The coloured skin ripens around its drop of sapience.

On the far side of the sun the lost radii
Spill the full-spectrum flows into the blind scape.
Unflected axes pulse across the waste of black sand.
Frayed, as an inverse square, the forlorn floods
Dissolve from iron to helium and again dissolve
Dissolve from helium to light and again dissolve
Rush on, break from a nova into a sea
From a sea to a flame
From a flame into a beam
From gleam into a chink
From a chink to a flicker of diffuse quanta.

Out in the pressureless heatless soundless reefs of carbon
Winks of light caress the skin of the blind beast
And sparks feel out the pupil of the blind orb.
In a dizzying reiteration of strict metre
The separation of light and darkness writes itself out.

*Skeletons Looking at Chinese Pictures* (1983-1987)

No light is lost or destroyed,
Just foundered;
For, strung out on the pallium of separation,
The rays outline a web of perfect distribution:
An image of awesome size
Without an image
Aswirl
Around the yolk of the flying threads.

## About Living Opposite the Brewery in Brick Lane

It floods and gushes
It sluices into the warehouses and markets
It billows up under the railway bridge
It floats in at the windows like a cloud

Is this me shaking in a drunken fog
Or is this the air in stupor rolling me?

If you walked (let's imagine) in a woodland
Designed with Arcadian sentimentality (I'm
not Zola), full of bees but not breweries,
Where a sea of wild hops grew on stumps and
Hedges, rambling over empty acres, snaking
Out where the competition had been levelled, teeming and shooting
and rioting
And creeping and sprouting and digging and swarming
And honking with that smell; and you fell
Right into that bramble, footless,
Dizzy, drowning in hops
Stirred up by the sun; that
Is what Brick Lane was like that night.

I lie in bed with my window open, gulping in
Effluent dreams, cloudy brain music,
Hop banks drifting across the moon...

The scene swims and shifts to SHEAF,
First of the English kings, the royal infant
Two thousand years ago adrift
In an open boat, wind-swept up
On some soft mud-flat in Frisia. The destiny
Of the Saxon race is tied to those plumes,
That spindlestraw, those unripe grains. Lo, he speaks.
"I am not a Middle Eastern fertility god"
Were his first words. Then,
"Primitive Communism is OUT". Then,

"Put me in a hole and pour water on my head".
The locals were out catching flounders with their feet.
Fore-Jutish oafs sank to their knees,
Ere-Angles blathered about the runrigs,
Crab-crackers did fealty, prone on the polder,
Yore-yokels felt the damp majesty of the moment:
"I delve the ditch my people delve,
I drink the ale my people drink;
*Waes hael* Sheaf! founder of dynasties!"

The noble, the tall, the potent King Barley
Swept away trees, scrub, and various boulders,
Turned strong men into wallowing pigs;
Organized hoeing, dibbing, reaping, and brewing,
Bureaucracy, the verb system, the family laws,
Metrics, the sharing of the harvest, cooking, the calendar,
Land drainage, runes, and public ceremonies.
Roll over that yeasty salt sea, Sheaf!
Let herrings do homage! let loyalist seagulls
Offer up their palpitating white bosoms to your teeth!
Hit the soggy Saxon shore like Montgomery! (Somewhere out there
Prince Flake, lord of salt,
Makes his way past holms and inlets
Across a sea of ale, where a light swell
Laps at his gunwales; and the lucent moon
Tilts the vast masses of liquor as if in a cup.)

The scene blurs and shifts, spun by a Drunken Sage.
Scattered on the floor of a warm barn,
The barleycorn sprouts in an illusory Spring,
Converting winter stores in wrong resurrection,
It seethes, it starts, it rocks and rolls,
It turns its larder to sugar, in the hazy oast;
And gets killed off with boiling water.
This sexual sturm-und-drang comes to no good.
Farewell, rash sprout...

The image fades, once more to clog.
In the glow of the sacred fires

Kindled from knotless and smooth-burning timber
Hand-lopped for even heat,
Wheat priestesses of the Northern Ocean
Mixed malt and barley, steeped them in fire and iron,
Infused poisons, drugs, and herbs,
Lit a slow casserole of roil and transmutation.
Three Kings bear gifts of hops and peaty water,
Twelve robed apostles turn the malt into beer.
Hocus pocus. The liquid bread shifts shape. They
Pour phials of corn-blight into it. Or something.
They fill the *calicem salutis perpetuae*,
The big vats foam up like Persil and it gives off gas.

By the open window
I roll in fitful unreliable dreams.
The Fen pores over my books,
The vapourware immerses my bedroom.
I scull legless in the suds of memory, the Barley Nebula
Forms a weak turbine in each perforation.
Slippery bines are draped from invisible poles
Opulent miasmas draught a smeary Beer Animal.
In Brick Lane
The mash surges through huge white canisters
Gleaming above the street
Like heads of foam,
Rushing and sluicing
Through the tangled internal works
Like the juices of winter and summer
Refluxing in the pipes of the world.
Spitalfields smells like a blooming wood.
Yellow light pours off the guttering,
Lamps flare up in the slag-rich raindrops.
Beer elevators load barges down on Limehouse Cut,
The street flows like a blind-drunk canal.

## The June Sun Cast as the Absent Lover

The embrace of the sun strips me and lays me out,
The warm clasp sliding across my skin
Is not corporeal and not affectionate.
Reckless and remote,
A shock of gold unshackles my limbs.
Nothing is so warm except blood.

I know your blood is strong, o sun, it fattens
A million grapes and wells upon the tendril
And gleams red when it is spilt; it rears like a beast
In the glass enclosure; its Syrahs and Tokays,
Its muscats and monemvasias,
Its tears and hazes,
Its flocs and drowses,
Irrigate your body.
I drink your cognac, o sun, I
Drink your Franconian wine in lacquer bowls, I
Drink your Lombard blossoms in a fragrant grove,
I replace my bleak blood with yours.
Your limbs are all of grapes, my sun;
Your skin is the sea flashing in the shallows.
I drink your summers, spirits, sugars;
I pass out in your milk of splendour.

Up there the Fall is still happening, the
Fragments of Paradise fall incessantly to the ground,
The wounded darkness loosens its clench,
Eden's unnamed florescence thrives for a threemonth.
Dark lines crackle your ingot, I see
Your face shaped, my love; I see your smile.
I know you for a second. Who are you?
Your compassion turns up my face where I live
In the sad darks.
Your beauty drops my eyes, your beauty
May I not sustain. Am I not pious?
Do I not wait for you? The berry

Is white unripened in the late season,
And I waited in vain for the sun.

You cause the skin to cry out loud, you repeal
The blindness of the limbs, they form images
In bright mass on their lolling pulp.
I lie here in the grass and listen
To the shapes stirring written across my body.

In the evening is repentance, the white
Petals of regret fall from the cooling sky,
The images of the day drift as memories into the North;
In the Morning
Is labour, the back bent in the harness,
The iron across the forge; the straight light
Envelops the curved edges of machines like a Zeiss lens,
There is neither memory nor fatigue.
Those are good hours.
Noon is the hour of love,
It beats like a bell in the heavens;
Noon is the shaft of love, the star flares
Cracking open on the blue hull of steel,
The zenith and arrogance of the day,
Its hungers, its flanks of meat, its gold cuirass
Strapping a gold back, its animals lowering
Their heads to drink; its
Wet blazes trickling out over the grass, the weight
Of mid-day pressing me down, softening my limbs.

I ripen myself in the torrent of golden drops, ropes
Of flax and linen hailing in motes and silence.
The sunshine is swallows ripened on a tree,
And the swallows are sunlight fledged and fleeced,
Cutting the fabric of the fine beamness.

I lucify myself with immensity and
Drench myself in density and
Glaze myself with gaudy gold and
Fleece myself with blazes of stellar velocity.

*Skeletons Looking at Chinese Pictures* (1983-1987)

## Shapeshifting and Mismatches

Look at the creatures. Their frames are like ours;
Their limbs are four; their blood, red; their eyes
Catch shapes in their rich and acrid water.
Our human husk is frail in its disjunction,
One fertile fire eats and casts shapes on and on.

Bone and plane the metal beasts writhe.
The shared mirror-images shift and parade
In the smoking mirror where fine wisps waft across the axis.
Trance axes slide: in furs and masks
We go through the beast-dance.
The masks' asymmetry fixes
The discordant halves of beast and man.
The eye-globes spot a stereometric mismatch;
Flawed overlay.
There is a start between the planes.
The writhing picture lashes and escapes.
The mirror-image stirs and walks away.
By night we run four-footed in the forest,
We run and run…

The repoussé die is brother of the foil it masters.
Every boss, a dint; every groove, a welt; reverse
Moulding in negative control.
The body bears the record of its smithing,
Axes eager to shear and swivel symmetry:
Arms to legs; right to left; ribs to spine-whorls;
Perception to world; eyesight to handstroke.
That is fine workmanship
In a good and pliant stuff.

On the brooch the bright beasts
Look like the Snake which broke and tined to Adam's form:
The ribs shooting from his dappled side
Hoop and pinion the tottering trunk:
You shall go upright, face the sky.

In bronze the limbs undergo new transforms.
The growth-plans of the body's symmetry
Talk to each other with dies and matrices
Like holes through which wires are drawn.
Twined and clotted from flesh and stone, mankind's frame
Cools in a burnished trance like this bronze tress.
On the wood the animals dance.

We steal the attributes of the beasts.
This hand causes extensions to my body;
This sword is my outer and earth-won fang.
This double-wool saffron cloak is my fleece.

Asymmetry finds and pours out new forms.
The two halves of a man's face de-matched
Compose the first lineaments of his son.
A net trawls shapes in the blood
From shoals teeming as herring, unlike and kin.
Let them refrain from bestial incarnation,
The grey fur of the son in the cradle,
The animals discoursing in human tongue.

# The Fallen Stone Tells the Poet How to Write

Jewels like eyes in the palace of Confinement. Worked stones fall out of the sky. The subsoil is pitted with dream objects. The hexagonal lattices, pack jewels, of the ice are hewn, hard edged, memories of the inexistent. The galaxy which is our unconscious nourishes its Nativity Animals. We delve and knead together huge letters out of clumps of mud and reed, laying out a Text readable from five miles up.

The rocket's track brings about the night, the swirring arrow gives birth to the sky. Orphans of an alien sky, wait for the candour of your star. Time is the product of the stars, the sky is hewn by projectiles.

I am the enemy of the Gods, the adorer of the stars. Starlight flecks my eye as I pack the snow into an ideogram. The workshop of telescopes builds rifling for the guns of light. Pictures disassemble for transport across the steppes of Space. Part patterns flicker in the dust eddies, the mouth of shadows utters a cosmogony of lies. Fragments tear the celestial envelope in both directions. Radiation and dust hoarsely emit virtual messages; strange cries from the death of matter. Disintegrated images from the reefs of vacant glare.

We mount the altitudes deserted by the gods. Gods were just my weakness and nymphs my concupiscence. The image parts to reveal the real sender; the firm illusion unwisps to give away the tenuous and shifting source. Star tines twine out the vexing shapes of neurosis; a boundless field of analogies sprawls in that glow like DNA. Pale seraphs depart with their summonses. Scorch tracks run down the side of the gantries. I spring into the eye of the Cosmos like the arrow which is the sparse tendon of the Unknown Waste.

I bow to the superior technology; I move towards the new metals. I pick up the fragments of an artificial star. I orient myself by the new mathematics. I spurn the dust of the pious regimen, I am scanned by the new velocity. I abandon my home; I surrender to the untapered flights.

I go in search of the finest data. I skid across the velocity barrier. On the sound surface, the vibration almost solidifies, waves peaking at the same point. Ripples eat into the hollow charge of fuel. The combustion is blowing itself out. The engine casing shakes as if it were boiling away. A tide cuts through the chambers of fire; a wave paradox tracing the contour of Mach-1, pinned across the Sonic Surface. A jagged explosion reveals the rhythmic nature of flame. The throat of fire seizes up and snares. Detonation ceases. The wave forms are carved into the unburnt charge like ripples in sand: memories of the Woolwich chemical fuel experiments in '43. You have to find the scansion of the oxygen tides; code in the numbers of fire. The shudders are tuned away.

## In High Places

Vavilov in the Pamirs
scaling the meson wakes across blacked-out silver
eye open in high places
as the dross falls away
the structure of matter is revealed

In the sparseness
gleaming flakes of truth lie under hand
the thick air acts as a blur

fragments of the cosmic substance
impinging at nigh-impossible velocities
skimming a wake in the emulsion
tagged for mass, speed, and bearings
flight paused to pure knowledge

Keen eyes search the blue flickers of snow
in the high wastes where a bard in tall lamb cap
wanders in a trance seeing and reciting.
In the pied coat of tatters covered in jangling iron
he climbs the mountain too high for birds to cross
by the path marked only by the bones of novice bards
to find the one to show him
everything which is above the earth or beneath it
everything which is in the past or in the future
drawn in the bronze mirror wrapped in black cloth.

Vernov already in 1934
releasing balloons too light to return
the particle impacts logged by telemetry

the new sensory skin feeling out the Utter, the high ranges

quitting the terrestrial as if ruling out corruption
before and above error
the unknowing knower

sheathed in lead and wired for radio emission
shoots truth out in radiant pulses
the messengers rarer than language

the difference between inner and outer wiped
the longed-for truth raining down on Vernov
from 15 miles out
severance repealed

fifteen miles
between Vernov and his fingertip
would the line be true?
in a frame where the earth is data corruption
and the heat of the eye is Error

in high places the unmediated bolts
tear holes in the mind
in the high wastes the poet wanders dazed and fabulating
by the roots of stars
would the spirit descend? would the fit destroy him?

awareness is a pulse
flicked across a backless mirror
in the tick of blanks and slats

motion limned but not caught
by a gleaming streak

the event scratched the graphic surface of silver
lips of the wake parted in the deep emulsion
ripple nuclei explode
crests summate to fray in light and foam
the vortex overloads its own patterns
the swimmer's hand pushes the water in the swimmer's shape
scanning of pulse peaks declares a buried star

*Alien Skies* (1993)

## Jadis j'ai cru

I once believed
We could make our home where in the large rooms
A smell of wax and flowers would fill the air
And, where music trembles and disappears
Along rolls of time cooped in the wood
You would have your wish.
Each word I hear slips
From those rooms, I know by its
Acoustics; as fallen stones prove by curve and working
To be heaven's rooftiles slid during a storm.
The words of poems dapple a vanished whole. A straight cadence
Lifted from the stream of presence.
Space bursts from around your body, close to you
Is everything I imagine or desire.

Out of thin air a voice composes
A glass palace of seven stories in a wet meadow
Of flowers scattered in flecks of blue and red
As if the callous tossing wind had seen a carpet pattern,
And grasses lush and springy to the foot,
This side of bog but sopping bright awash in Spring, poured
By a river of sweet water where we swim
Down walls between blue rock falls
Or up still green-padded creeks snagged by willows,
Or across broad flat reaches to the islands;
Conducted in channels of human art,
Through mirrors of trees bowed by weight of apples,
Where the slow hum of wasps slows to show
The thief nuzzling at the sun in the flesh.
Below, winding off the mush of pulpy apples,
Split, slackened, soil-crusted, on the turn,
A heady smell reminds me of coarse strong drink.

I went across the river

As day inclines and breaks in colours
*an claidheamh soluis*
The reddish sword of light
Catches on the webs and fine moisture of the meadow
Walking along the tips of grass-blades and clovers
Where gossamer or rain or floss or first dew
Twine a net of reflecting surface
It shimmers in darts where the wind moves along it, refracts,
And the sword
Writes a broad shining track.
The attendants slight the palace of the day
To draw the groundplan of the fort of night.
On the municipal playing field
Just where the Wood Brook enters the town
Walking along light threads
I fold up my cloak of lies; slight breaths
Falling like petals from the heady inane.
I imagine what I lack.

Night wears its tints through, another day wipes dry
The visible from the thorough vapours of darkness.
Falling mingling with the sunlight we hear
The second language, not that
Which changes with the nations and the coasts
And sullies with each fleck of distance and matter,
And dies as its wave form dissipates, instead that other
Which is universal and immense and
Is spoken by the heart, audible
In summers and on mountains and by moonlight.
What is to fire as fire to wood?
Or what colour is the horse of air
Which carries birds in the direction of our longing;
I found its track in ashes and ruins
Whether
In some Northumbrian love song like 'I drew my ship'
Or in an Appalachian ballad dubbed from an old 78
Rustic chivalry slowly set out in courtly state
To adorn the beauty of a farm girl
Or at the named moment

When patterns overlay and match
In a woman's face turned towards me.
It's just an old song I misremembered.

A span out of the fundamental structure of space.
As during exile
As a child who had to live in homesickness
My voice was part of what I had lost and I
Froze it to keep that sound from contagion
Now silence is my part but I still remember
The house of large rooms.
My family appeared by intermittence, light
Shone right through it when it was there.
I kept faith in carceral conditions.
Ruled by an idea at nine years old
I learnt then how to be an artist,
Kept warm by the intangible and
Fed sleek and fat by the unreachable.

Split between two places I am half now
Of what you want to possess
You seize on my intermittence
And I can't paint across the gaps
I can't build that house.

# Circular

A noise comes off the highway
From the metal plates shaking
Numbering the surface of waste energies;
From the hot pipes of the steel throat
In the pinned fabric of motion
The sound rushes across the road shore & rims.

Blast apron
Hard sound over the inadequates
In the pitted surface of the media slew
In the middle of eight million faces.

The motorized column covers its section of loop.
The messages were effaced.
A citadel of numb skin,
Signs arrested
Rooms in the throb of fuel chambers.
The specific metallic signal,
Shivering and blowing away words,
The unwriter of thoughts & patterns.

Along the rims
A certain group moves in to low prices.
They don't understand the signals too well anyway,
It doesn't matter.
You memorized the map that got you here.

No escape by eating transit. A swarm glutted & limed
On foodstuff, stampede of cars
Going round and round between close walls,
Lost migration on the Lost Highway.
One-way passage down the throat of insensate words
Laminar sounds peaking to blank uproar
Movements overlaying to a complete circle.
This is the message you were built to hear.
Look for a crack.

## Roots of a Revolution

In the stasis of fearful energies I flip out unconscious
Twenty thousand people fired and I've made a career.

A head stream of dark air. The world buckles
We represent it, gritting our teeth and closing our eyes.
Some people can't even see it and
Ah! we see every trait!
Why the ships cross the seas
Why the reactors burn
Why the shortages and what shapes the flesh is worn into.
We see a sense that marshals events
From the pipes of Siberian gas
To the waiting lumber of Brazil
From the cracking vapour of the refineries
To the trays of goods hawked in the supermarkets.

Look traveller at this site
An island on the edge of the ocean waste
Wharf space plus warehouses plus finishing shops
They live by buying and selling each other.

A comb of scant living spaces; the metaphor
Of a ship: a rope's end and cramped berth on
A trading venture. Sailors overseeing slaves
And officers sailors. Every inch reckoned and
Bodies fitting in those inches. Movement banned.
Fingering the trade goods down in the hulk.

Why are the crowds running in the streets?
A fit has afflicted the people of the island
They stand out on the moor in thousands
Tearing at their heads till the blood flows and tearing,
Expounding Scripture and chanting sales slogans
Mumbling broad paternosters and thieves' rigmaroles

Imitating a leader as he barks like a dog,
Focuses on thin air, washes water with clay,
Scribbles copies of till rolls on waste paper,
Eats leaves, wearing pans tied to his wrists,
Clutches bundles of rags and pours lye on scabs.
Pressing together till the middle is crushed,
The envelope of flesh overflows.
A red dragon lashes among the crowds,
Ten thousand flour weevils move in step behind a leader,
A headless horse gallops over the moor,
Its body is fleshed and ribbed with our mania,
Racing in a sweat to turn a mill
It breaks up our homes.
Thousands of pilgrims are selling their houses
They are rushing south and tearing away north
And none could say where he was going to.

The factories are empty and the streets
Are full of sleeping people.
Simply that their last inch was stripped.
Their minds revert to the other space, the boundless featureless.

Goods piling up in the halls, the lorries
Never pulling out. Too much inventory.
The drivers cold with standing, drifting
In and out the office. All out of destinations.
We serve as many as will
Whoever they are, boys,
They won't take our gear,
Their will is free where relationship is compulsion,
Whatever's in their homes
It's foreign or they don't have no homes.
Rig your sails by the weather.
Cut your prices, take in your throat.

Quick capers tow row a brave cotillion
Danced to a far spectator
Somewhere in EC2, or in a Washington front office
Tossing hands to my head with trained gestures

*Surveillance and Compliance* (1987-92)

Dwarfed by remoteness
Please please please

I count timings and outputs
A footsoldier of the New Right
A Black Guard of the repressive revolution
A shantyman of the speedup on the line
Marshal of group motion.
Enforcing the new norms. Locating the waste
To pare off, even be it of organic form,
In two shoes. Don't you understand
If you can make the speed
You don't have to die?
There is no because in group illusion
It's an outburst of hatred, a communal violence,
It's like religion it's like war. A shared game,
A ritual excitement, under drums and herbs.

Why are people dying in the streets
It's part of the price mechanism,
As an expression of human wishes
Whose aggregate is you die in the markless space.
It's part of the sin mechanism
It's an organ of State.
The tall buildings are empty;
Waste under the arches and in the underpass.

A fit that drove me for those years
Like burning ashes in my hand.
Ask what skills I mastered,
Precise knowledge modelling the universe.
Ask, what passions worked me,
What kind of man was this and what faith this was,
What fits and appetites in my body:
This dream—winch the norms up.
The screw turns another notch. My arms knot and rip.
My mind beaten soft.
I wiped my ideas, slept
Beneath my lathe. I wanted to get the goods out the door

And keep the factories open and
I cut the water with a knife.

Tell me I was never there
Tell me my awareness is provincial errors
Tell me human awareness is unwarrantable
Tell me I wasn't part of the group I belonged to for nine years
Tell me I wished for this to happen
Tell me not to empathize.
Rationalize my words
Rationalize my memories and my emotions
Rationalize the society I belonged to.
Illuminate, turn, and erase.

## The Policy of Weakness

You get the picture, a china jug in 17 pieces, cell and cowl,
slashed fuel lines, frost on the can, desertification,
setting fires under water, stilled flattened framed, yes we see.
Put a frame round it. Mutilate it. Rant and rail.

When I first met Mark, he said I needed a piss
in a pub by Euston Square, a bag of white stuff
was behind the knuckle of the pipe that made me
blush to my collarbones. Thousand mile stare. So
I came back to this ruin of ruinous livelihood.

Midnight on the wharf of the glass sea, rain on the leaves of the summer trees
The infrared stores of the stacked bricks wash through the billows of rain
enclosed space
modulated by four people
around a tumbledown room near the multiplex of railway tracks
as the night sets sail from the green shores of the Grand Union Canal

Chill swirrs from the blue interiors of foliage
Two talkers, high on ideas.
How false I feel smothered in the skirts of your
big opulent durable feelings, your
so fluent and false intuitions of Being
setting sexual lures. Mark yarns about dealing in Liverpool. While I

*dans les plâtras de mes combinaisons écroulées*
the spinner of a formal span that rots in neglect and darkness
am crushing dust into stone and flesh into dust!
sumptuous flourishing piers, on paper only,
tender skin ridged with swelling and fever.
Decidedly my enterprise is ready for commissions
I have no debts no stock and no policy.
If there is leisure one has to do things without motive.

In a stupor straining to measure what to conform to
in the room but not in the script, smiling

vague and like a viper in shock
I pour every drop into the broken cup

She was a pilgrim on the Bad Drug Way from Keele to Camden,
she wants to be a teacher and they won't let her near their kids
she wants to be a faith healer and cuts reason away
some anecdote about psilocybin, hospital, and lung damage
she's got five voices coming out of her head and
she is filled with yearning by my new Soho haircut

a mirror for demons, a snapshot of depth
the gaze which captures and reads
uncovered surfaces could find out my weakness or
acquire personality traits by imitation
I can't read the signature of these events
in the picture of desire fulfilled and lofty souls that
tell me what controls me and
try to scoop me up like ice cream. Smooth swatches,
sex talk, display, blinding glint of words, it's
the strong against the weak.

After scenographic shimmering floods of anxiety
the act of identification caught and cut into frames,
proteins freeze as glass. Passionate
white powder. A shocked hurt thing that turns and turns
and has no body
hand on mouth choking on involuntary knowledge
faced with the music but not rising to dance
A lyric poem without a hero who in a clean room
opens the filters to engorge the objects of
long persistence and toxic effect
on frail native tissue. How much I admire
the pylon throb of your feelings in which I deploy
mimic response. You mistake my silence and apathy for
sweetness of character. I rise to go.

Streets hosed with hissing yellow light.
Planning Monday's shift in my head.
Singular matrix error at hex address 74B791

*Surveillance and Compliance* (1987-92)

No response from logical unit 128
Pictures going down the data line to Harlow
through stages and under the earth.
Do you know what a singular matrix might be, Ruth?
Do you think two geometries might not fit and engage
gushing down the dark channels of this summer night

# Heat Loss

A rippling shimmering shrilling scream
lacerates the blue air
my teeth sneering in rictus
my hands shake with its thrills.
in the pit of the gullet
where all voices are drowned out
those little wishes of so many millions

through the factory gate
one pile of goods, one of consciousness.
a tally on the blue slips
Surveillance's means of thinking.

A man I wished to be
watches me from the window of a hotel.
His eye crushes me. I can't walk.
The energy frame ripping my arms
from my back. The colours and forms
dissipating.

The soul and the illness share the body
cohabitation under long clauses
the illness has all the outside world

Just for a door to keep the world away
I sell my precision and cease to perceive.

What animals what trees
what cold mountains and gushes of sweet water
what riders in black robes picked out by white discs of mail

Illusion deprives the senses, trauma as coping
keeps fantasy from dispersing
cherished and fettered and pent and flattered.
I'm falling out of a glaze of suppression,

nothing has changed or faded;
turning again to run through the rustling forest

Each path is spun out of one apex
planes out of shadows
finger running down edges
tracing outlines in roiled waters.
at the edge of the area
are latches to unlock it

I made myself a poet
wishing nothing else
as without power you know nothing.
The silence stands for what I know,
the white noise
drills in my ears
I can't hear a single lucid syllable.

Working up
in the markless repetition of anxiety
for a decisive violence
to smash whatever can be ripped out.
The books
written in red and black letters
describe operations of exit: the undoing
of the architecture.

slick pliant film
NATO spec fineness
tissue regions richly filled
with the glaze
modelling the inanimate
still receptors

a shimmer of heat leaving the body
detached plane
is exit line
coloured pane

# At Camden Lock

The control gate opens to destroy a state
the dark water wells and thrashes
8-foot cascades sheer fall white gush
white tracks muscling the wet saurian
eerie cambers of smooth curved glass
ebb to raindrop ripples of pencil-thin
the eye searches for meaning on wan waters
as if the energy had a body.
the debris of the market resurfaces
the fairway silts up

From the first you watched your family as if from darkness
Immersed in the dense material cinema
Father, mother, restrictive lease
You pieced together numb words and speaking objects
Thousands of days left a taped regime.
Now, you wish it will never be again. Holding
A word beneath your tongue
That has no people and no things, you
Look for a place to be the outer of it.
Sighting the program to a string of numbers
You transform, shifting as their values shift
x to x' y to y'.

Among penguins and marmots, a row of monkeys
Of a dozen species, I saw each one
Fiddle with the lock or the bolt,
Imitating human fingers.
Every control gate has a fastening.
They go through what acts are possible without a forest.
I make a mental model of this special geometry.
Symbols unlatching edge of pattern cycles.

A thieves' market for chemicals clothes art and lovers.
A sluicy libido rides on complex order
Pushing everything out through the surface.

*Surveillance and Compliance* (1987-92)

Everybody I love can be dressed here
Everything I want can be found here.
A self in the white net of the body in
The sliding planes
Shopping for missing parts.

You lie down with such travelling people who
Lose the knowledge which confines them
That was reality and your desires.
Through the erasing heads, under the darkness;
Who take you like a drug and speak a ritual
And soak in your words and looks and caress;
Who lie because memory is a shackle and
Look you in the face and do not know you.

Torpid then, sated. swelling spent. slacken and loll.
Sleek black pressure head lounging towards the curl
shotglass chutes mirror rushes battered foam
under the sleeks of moss where splashes spent their course
gin yards, translucent turbine.
aligned between blue brick coamings
contact zone chokes and babbles white
flung free foamflecks dry

## Tuyau as heat lens

blind cones focussing crushed light
falling in. ray becoming solid object.
a convergence of straight lines
beating the universe into a pattern
by a distortion of the inner organs
seizing an emotional property, tapering
trapping past and future in a hot solid.
mesmeric certainty. asthma. fever.
furnace throat blocking up.
breathe in the ash pit, blow
those supple flakes. strophes of
prophetic rage. cells turgid, swashing heat.
cult division and private code
an interpretative school. an autonomy.
rigid with message, clenched with destiny
uttering irrevocable gold charges
a hysterical cone burning what it swallows

a ripple of chill
as your inside disappears
and a remote stable world stretches itself out
in four directions
signless shapeless selfless
ochre field
        like the ash
                of a lost paranoia

The lens with a thousand parts
is disassembled  waste light
wringing out of it in rolls
The bursting of the cell wall
the loss of precious inner narratives
of knowledge and an idea of character
The loss of cinnabar, pine resin, and medlar pulp
the inner waterways

*Surveillance and Compliance* (1987-92)

so numerous in their openings
so rich in dissolved substances

A room of glass cases
A face that slips away
storing relics of wholes that never existed
a slab of inlet fossils
clean sliced and polished high
A sequence of words
scored in an image complex
tapering to the furnace shoulder

# Shiny Circuitry

Mark worked for five years in a hi fi shop,
he merged into those shiny tiny furls of
coupled cavity loading, dither quantisation masking,
explicit lateral and depth imaging, subtle spatial clues,
horizontal glass plates flecked to break up surface standing waves,
jewel tip heated to several hundred degrees,
turntable members sizzling with suppressed whoosh,
pitless balls running in a countersunk, highly polished mirror, lost
signal buried in the null excess of the noise floor,
learnt the guitar; disappointed,
he hadn't realized that art involved feelings,
he thought clarity and sonority
CLARIT
Y
SONORIT
Y
were the end of it.
Stored with numbers
and the distinct states of equipment, couldn't
process insight and feelings: when
two signals fight over one sound stage.
Fussed by the unmeasured. Gave up the guitar.
Testing the jolt and grain (as we call it) of industrial chemicals,
he uses his whole nervous system
as a layer of self-organizing components,
circuits and output devices, to thrash at high gain.
The miracles of science in your home! such a shame
representing other people hindered
the high-brilliance solid send of libido.
Am I going to tell him
that the "human" works or can be relied on?

And art is pure. Rhys' painting shows
young men larking in a bathroom of some hotel,
where a plume of steam laps the flanks of silvery pipes
standing for the whole kit of urethra, spongiosa, veins, glans,

*Surveillance and Compliance* (1987-92)

that squalid tap and bottle
he'd spent so many hours over
so many times. Soap foamed. A pleasing flow
sluiced through the conduits banded
by massive hoops. Memories, of course,
of shower stalls at school, and those temples
of rusty pipes, dark walls and basic scrawls
where brothers met over hydraulic concerns.
Deep rococo conches filled with languor,
marble facings where a pure pearl chills out and drips.
Let's not dwell on the tone values
of clean (for dirty), metal and ceramic (for flesh), stiff
(for sagging), constant flow, steam, brightness.
How much I despised that painting.

## Fragments of the Above

She looks up at the coast dipped in glare,
an island as if one washed by the sea
slowly enveloping the extent of the sky.
A moment hangs in the air
between raising her foot and setting it down,
and she watched her own figure, passing along the shore,
completing actions

The street is closed in a thin glass cube,
the pulses so slow they leave wakes,
of imitation taking speech and gestures, like clothes
draped on the racks of the Market, completing
their actions. Patterns copying themselves,
columns converging on the place to be,
adornment redividing the light splashing off the body,
like a spray of surf flashing.

The moment freezes.
Every diagonal stands out like a track on a circuit board.
T-beam stanchions of observation platforms beside the raised way
blue pipes of scaffolding against the railway bridge
rivet-headed braces of the bridge bulkheads
windlass and key of the lock winding gear,
that moment dissolves and exhales.
Everything you want can be found here. A girl
swirling past my sight in Harlequin clothes;
the vortices of the market make my blood rush.

The swirl of flakes of the island tumbling
rippling, darkening, glittering
falls out of the sky over Camden High Street
*the only happiness I know or can know.*

It did come out of the sky, a tile
from the roof-ridge of the Exterior.
Filmy wings in your hand, ash

clogging in the storm-drains along Chalk Farm Road,
clings to the knots of your sweater.
You shake and eddy and blow away
a dust wave, a swirl of separate flames,
hull drawn from spiral trails
breaking up in the light it spills

You can't find your hands.
In the downfall—
*The Sibylline will be Mine, its Gift of valid Prophecy*
*An Eye not Carnal moves in and out of Time*
*I Drink of the Living and Dead waters*
*The Drugs I Take shall free All Men—*
under the general downfall of flakes bearing words,
a long fuselage blown across sunbeams and aimless smoke
between the Lock Market and Jamestown Road Workhouse,
its pieces fluttering past our hands, your mouthfuls of gnosis
whose dispersion is the stutter of your words.
Tip them as they fall
try to catch a life's worth

# At Cumae
*Cumae 1987*

Whatever I know is carried away on the breeze
Blowing from the throat of the rock, where the wells
Of light are cut into the cold hill.
Sibyl of a hundred voices, what is my fate?
Sibilate
Whatever places whatever bodies
Whatever pleasures and whatever longings
Will be mine

The blue lash's drift of susurration
Lifts besides yours. Sea of winejars sheet of copper
Sea of chance! That medium
In which men fall like dice through air
Or drugs through flesh
Borne up and pinned down
Washed through the strophes of an unmoved voice;

And by the edge, at its warmest and filthiest,
Where heads swim at the gulls' diving-place
Sailors consult the women of the harbours,
Salt skin chapped in the frayed sparrage and cords of the night;
Behind the wharves, the red stews and daubes,
Campanian wines with a putrid edge
Divide the days of exile
And the women foretell love and voyages,
The cold bony jaws of fish,
Seeing too far into the patterns of the flesh.

I am uncertain, crone who looks out from stone lip,
Whether I will ever possess human flesh again,
Knowing it with the rule of my hands
Tugging it into position and vanishing in that place
As vessels burst in my head like strong wine
Driving the blood in lashings against the skin

*Uncollected* (1991-1996)

Rearing welts and engorgements on a white drape.
Tell me, tell me true

Lingering on the sumptuous torn fruits of the South
Has my soul left my body and lost its way?
Or on the rim where the sun's drops freeze as amber,
In the whorled unreadable tracks of the Northern darkness?

The forces lock till awareness is lost.
Ships ventured too far into the hatred of the stars
Warm bodies lapped in the cold mineral blood
Crawling in the shallows where the water shines like tin
Heartbeat fading in the reckonable tide

I have foreseen too much. My fate is blank;
The breezes blur and hiss a hundred syllables,
Run through the many holes in the cliff
Modulating and delaying
As if a throat's curve in living rock
Spoke words
In a primitive language
Before knowledge and from where the waters come,
The heart caught on air as if a face on a mirror
Lifted out of the broken surface of the self
Where an eye might see many moments as flashes, paused
To turn motion into shape.

I hear parts of many sounds
Perhaps the surf, perhaps my blood beating or
A message. A heap of fragments.
What do you want. What do you want.

# Three Graves

*1. Kurgan : Kostromskaya. 500 BC*

The tempering is complete.
Oracular sparks
From a forge up by the sun.
The pure gold weapons falling out of the sky,
the *Khvarenah*, the aura and luck of the family,
sign out the founder of the dynasty.
Nearby the Slav villages thrive without lords, the mir
of wooden ploughs, of wattle and daub gaily painted,
nurture buckwheat and honey, know only
concrete living people who can be loved.
They lose the land: metal and horses
prevail over the plain in a new order,
in a scream of lording power.
In the frame of solid timber struts and studs
beneath a barrow the size of a hill,
the prince's rays of dominion
pass through a company of slaves and horses
in points of a geometry proven in corpses.

The eagle strikes the deer's back, cold hammered intersection
at kinetic maximum driven into a buckle.
Strike, javelins and chariots, interceptors
prolong the malice of the killer;
mechanical power
twisted up, held, in the bowstring, in the tendons
of the clan animals who bestow land: accoutrements
adorn the cavalry with speed and death.
Fierce and bloody-muzzled beasts,
given off by the lords' self-image, string the arc of the State,
trap with a new velocity. How did they range
from Silesia to the Siberian plain?
The chasers and smiths of fine-wrought trinkets
begin what we call Culture; the chattels of noble households.
The names of kings
begin what we call History.

The killers of men lie under mud and jewels.
Five hundred barrows cluster beside rivers
as if hoping for the flow of chill infernal channels
to sweep the soul back from its penury.
The gold cup breaks. A new Sign cracks,
falling, Northern ice and starts a trickle of flesh.
Tyrfing.
Following where flocks of wolves and ravens led,
the Goths shatter the Scythian grip; a gold sword
lost and gained across the endless plains of fortune.
Ermanarich, Attila
muster steppe tiumens to subvert the Roman order.

Horses turn on a spit of wood; thill, axis, earth-pin.


## 2. Totenburg : Kutno. 1942.

The land over which a shout reaches:
here part the fields.
Here the Forebears cut the sod. The sowers of space,

wraths of the boundary. Hunters and interdictors
eviscerated by death, occupy their sons,
exude the line of rights. Bone trophy, title deed
of stone: palaces for the fallen
to weight the chord of State. Overlooking the Aryan land.
Son reared a stone upon the grave-mound:
sword glinted in the darkness, the wraith's meat cache.

Reconnaissance units
eastwards glimpsed the Caspian Sea:
the shores of the Aryan myth. The heartland.
Summer, 1942. At limit.

*Landnahme*
land frozen in overweening fantasy,
to pen women and workers in and rear sons.
Everything that can be seen can be possessed.

Race as resurrection, the killers of men
reborn through loyal passive flesh,
bequeathing on rights. The Romanesque harkbacks
claim Greek ancestry: a timeless idea
captured and reared in Germanic patrimony,
for example, in the Tomb of Theoderic or Ottonian churches.

Signed Wilhelm Kreis.
A poet in stone. Straining power right into his art:
He wasn't a whore; because he believed in this killing,
the building brigade driven by blueprint and whip
stands for the new society: the "Germanic order-giving strength";
breeding the Ukrainians as serfs,
taught self-contempt, to stoop and dig and haul:
a colony in the lying cosmos of power.

So: the rustic ashlar of the First Reich, the Ottonian;
censers where fat and bone might smoke in ghost-greed;
a naked sword as land-right. Overlooking the river.
His stones heaved up in visible power, citing
Death as a warrant to property,
snag and jag the border line:
Silesia, the Rhine, the Atlantic shore.
The Volga bankside monument was never built.

Oh, shivering eye-wounding fleshless sign
a distortion in Nature, a fever;
figures flower with icons of Blood and State
as if human memory bore such a burden
or human eye could believe such a message.

From the White Sea to the Caucasian crag
they marched East like small stones falling into deep water.
The men in black cloth and silver skull-flashes
summon death bindingly and by name,
admit His ordeal, rot at His attainder.
Their name is slight in the memory of Kursk,
the Black Sea gave up no leavings of the Seventeenth Army.
Hallucination taught them its order of march,

mutilation made them flinch.
Blood and soil mingling in a comrades' cup,
poured in libation swallowed in deep draughts,
where a Slav army triumphed, by a generation of spectres:
drugged by lies, outwitted, outgunned, lost:
they came too far and they stayed too long.


### 3. Sarkofag : Chernobyl, 1986

They wished to change human nature.

The prince lies in state in the secrets
of the earth, in the coves of the sky
among the precious jewels and crystals,
the special silicates never before realized,
and 180 tonnes of uranium, at Reactor Number 4.

The brave willingly piled this barrow: 17000 tonnes,
three chambers deep into the Ukrainian land,
and, like a smoke plume, sixty metres high.
The tyrant in his resurgence crypt,
lapped in the windings of signs constraining Nature,
schemes to re-occupy flesh, to parch
the gene lines of his enemies, and rear new fantastic breeds.
What happened to the German POWs in the Silesian pits,
to the zeks in the uranium mines of Magadan?
A new pulse occupied the offenders against the sovereign,
as if human flesh could eat those precious rays.
Honey will change, buckwheat will nod with a new head.
The explosion of the secret, secure, and supreme
writes finis to a regime of lies.
The monumental stele of a ruling class
rises to blurt out the proofs of Leninism.

In the Slav villages
the State gives the land back to the people.

# For C.

Like water falling through water.
Searching round your mouth for words.
Where does it hurt? it hurts in other people?
why do they hurt you? to prove their strength.
A jag of noise. Setting fire in ashes.

Write me a poem.
Make far things near, call cold things warm.
Why would I tell you lies
To violate your senses once again
going round your reason, mocked by others?
We'll see those bricks split streaming into fire and clay,
someone's going to hold you up and comfort you
this green you see is not the real green,
and I'm the same one who wounded you.

You know of that place,
of its long skies and jealous victors, of
the Cambridge air which made us ill.
They construct a desert in order to own it and
empty the senses in order to steady what they think.

They took your distress
and tried to prove how much they knew about psychiatry.
They tried to own your illness
and disproved what you thought
and refuted what you felt and
that's the kind of man I am.

Those fabulous serpents from Cambridge gardens
are quick to strike and cold to the touch.
Their venom is specific to human flesh, it makes
the tongue cleave to the neck, the aperture snicked to.
Its authority rests on silence.
When sated with food,
cold locator with hinged skull,

it prophesies in those rare tones, laying out
in linked symmetrical polygons
concentric precincts of derision and denials
to appraise the world of its expertise.

A tourist gawp, a painted sign
A bloodstained yard
where the Cutter superintends the repression of the repressed.

An instant before separating, before limbs and apparel, before
power flows out of the stone patriarchs, out of
the royal privileges, into the bottles on the trestle
table, and real hands, real mouths open.
The poised teenagers feint and engross
ready to blind with closed hands in the sorites
why someone goes away dry.
An instant before the instant before.

The eye focusses on the innocent body
until every inch of skin starts to itch
and the kempt surface slips and twitches in anxiety,
the gaze never inflects or responds,
the body jerks, folding up, looking for its own flaw
as if it could tear itself into a steady orthogonal
and the Eye closes to capture that snapshot.
The reticulations on the sighting lens make it Knowledge,
precise optics unsullied by shaking distress
and where the sight-wires cross, the candidate is known:
they don't want any of you.

You asked me for the consolation
of the only skill I ever wanted or called my own
in the wreck of your career at twenty-one
and the illness eating at your head
but I thought that someone soft and trusting
only needs a town to be oppressed
and only the stare of other people to be struck down again.

II

a blemish
a stain
where internal fluids seep out in public
dirty girl
a scab for them to pick out in session:
every time you started to mark the paper it stopped.
Your poems, surveilled too scared to speak. Thoughts picked their way
    between learning their speech in silence,
a panelled acoustic of angry tears,
lustre of attention and shrill shakes.

Why should you speak
to be chivvied where the Fellows of a querulous brotherhood
in small pockets finger keys to secret doors.
Why should you break silence, weaponless
where the air itself is inauthentic,
where the hush of the listener listening for the contours of weakness
colour-codes the zone of humiliation.
In the regional speech conduct that wiped ideas and feelings; *inmota*
    *orthonomia,*
your silence is the fulfilment of their training.

Grey noise, white void.
The poems you did not write of the Cambridge poetic school
are a sound reaching in the lipless for the out sign.
The shift from concrete to abstract
wrote off your experience as provincial.
The growth from subjective to objective
wiped out your feelings as messy and shameful.

You asked me for a poem
as if amongst that hell of ambition, of the novice
lips snapping at the sacral tones, and the young men
in a rage of vanity, going red in the face to
pick the crows of subtle cavils plume by plume;
as if where callow rulers
mastering the order of norms and testing,

*Uncollected* (1991-1996)

pick up the turn of phrase;
where hierarchy calls itself knowledge and
inadequacy is taught, learning the bounds and barriers,
I was good true or kind.

I upped to speak
And even as I mouthed the words
my blood poisoned me
with a slight crystal fury long of attainment.
Each image I framed went cold and died.
I had an idea of the poem I couldn't hear,
beyond what I ever wrote.
When you asked me for the very thing I wanted to give
that's when I foresaw
I had the gift of making someone unhappy.

To heal, or at least
catch the sight and motion of things healing.
I know that sick flesh can make healthy flesh.
Seeds blow on the wind and drop on every empty space
in idiot profusion; all ideas die
while the senses let in the swathes of light
and the pain has no defences. Yet
I wiped out the actual, strained at the blind edge to see
a superordinate darkness.


III

Too working-class. Too feminine. Too conformist.
They inspect every word in silence
pulling out every inch of knowledge like a worm from a hole,
taking every one as a symptom, you're fixed still
as the lad upright eyes front with the drill-sergeant stooped sharp,
turning his belt brasses over looking for a blue fleck
or a pinhead of polish not wiped off.
You went into the examination hall
through pipes of specialist glass guided by local impurities
where the Institution thrusts its novices into their class

and in the middle of the desks you
fell over in an epileptic fit.

Pulled by an emotion like a crack through the head,
the last defence of the self, last rally
tearing the nervous system into rags.
And this was your wish to conform at work.

They sell pain to buy pleasure.
The barrier that makes you unable to say no
rears in rooms where your wishes are excluded
and misused in carnal exchange. A voice
too gentle to fight for sensual reward,
on the pitch where the war to impose feelings
is won by withholding empathy:
a silence bought by one man
to be used by others.
You have no feeling which is yours.

It is written
they attempt an artificial death through mortifying;
they kill all corporeal powers, wipe out
all those influences that colour the (pure) idea in several ways; and
the Word flickers over the ascetic.
They suppress the reports of the senses
deleting and recording the deletion.
They despise the young
and bestow that as their trade.

On any flat surface
two vibrations contend
a shape emerges
which I pick up as my face and voice.

1979. I had three readers, and two were out-patients.
All I had to do was make bread feel like bread.
Tell us it, tell us it. No, again.

## Wind and Wear in Aix-en-Provence

A worn part of the sky has been dismantled.
The coping-stone from the tower in the Knights' Church,
Flanking the gutter where the celestial waters drained,
Was winched down and laid here in the yard: worn
(Soft golden flesh) by the centuries on guard;
Pitted, sodden, blown, gnawn, rubbed;
Rewarded with shape for its lack of resistance.

The raspberry on the earth-trailing branch
Lifts to reveal the moth: a cluster
Of fruits impaired and pierced, half lost
Half transformed into the robber, wings draggled,
Sleeping in black veils under the red riches.

And me, soaked and soluble,
Where experience's jags
Fret the pure quadrilateral of omnipotence,
I am replete and steeped. Pattern
Is the ruins of time; and time is feasting on us.

Flakes of transience glint,
Words, like fruit, light likenesses scattered
Over fairways. To speak is to wear the air,
To impart to the soft pouring medium all falling
Shapes. A wind pours steadily from the Alps and
Is part of their being; the mountain
With its scarf of air
Is contoured by abrasion. The
Universe is edible; the universe eats
Living stone to dessert on airy men.

Beside the channel where waters pour
The boundary is overwashed on both sides;
Breached on a micro scale; pores distend its skin
As if the fluids of sensation lapped at it.
Edges impart to pulp a contour.

Too many sides or too few.
Coloured scales leafwise on a counterpane.

The Torch Bearer who opens the lid of dawn
Inverts his Torch to close the rim of day;
A shifting boundary parts the opposed Twins
The glinting crown of Presence, bright sickle,
Strip of transformance, THE THIN REFRACTOR.
Objects double
To cross that bound, possessed and eaten up
Only to change the body which
Perceives, clasping within eyes or jaws,
So wraps an outside and breaks it,
Into error and vanity and self.

The sun's edge is not up there,
But deep within the earth, where the living surface ends;
I stretch my edge
Out on visible radiance to where the fruits are,
I get close to the universe by eating it.
The mind is a boundary, sickle wing
Dragged through objects as they flash by.
They are sopped and sullied in my mouth,
A splash of vapour both into illusion and forgetting.
Those colours favour what governs my eyes,
Parts of the plan of fruit-trees;
Fruit wrapped in colour as
A lure for clever simians, fed by the tree
To broad-cast its pips all amain across.
The tree memorized my longings long ago,
Expecting sun nitrates and monkeys. Midway
Between the absolute transience of light
And the sonority of massive stone,
The flickering solidity of animates,
Mounted on a moving tower
The gaze flicks through momentary horizons,
Sprayed by pulses of light.

Every pattern is wear and erosion,
Each one is completed by the scanner's death.

Moth and wind have gained their shares in me,
Each line of division lets fluids pass.
Sounds may fly when my carcass dies,
The apple is falling when it starts its flight.

# Martyrdom and Triumph of Sergei Korolev

The year is 1938,
The slave states glut on their gold and steel,
The entities of rage eat the living faces.
If the few forgot,
In the projects of lies and homicide, if they lost,
Faint, vengeful and overcome,
Part of the sparse lines of civility, stripped and chilled,
Stricken from the senses,
Who could bring it back?

Where the Kolyma River flows towards the Northern Ocean;
In the Zone of crime and atonement
Korolev dreamed of the paths to a new world.
In the astronomical belt of scarcity,
The staging zone towards metabolic
Death, spectres dig for gold in frozen soil. Where
The planet ceases, the cosmos
Trails its meshes of death and variation.
A nacelle streaks across Arctic skies.

Where minds must go first, K.
Dreams the divisions of fineness.
The stardown is wrapped and protected by their
Weightless reckoning, sensory planes peeled away,
Sheared, pegged, attenuated
For the serials of a new mechanics.
Body images
Falling through the reds and yellows of dawn;
A forest grows metal hulls,
Birch shafts shot through the track of the upper air.
He launches his fleets and watches their chances
Wiped in thousands, the error trailed and netted in the other sky.
His upshot makes a gravity wall loose as sand.
The nozzle is a muzzle of waste heat;
In a vacuum, it adjusts the course.
Like spires, minarets, columns, AA shells. A

Principle of ascent smooths and tapers the dream object.
Like earths, charcoal ovens, blast furnaces, breeches, bombs:
Chambers into which substances flow, and where they change.
The planet of sound, the Mach-1 surface, the tune of discharge
Resonance, singing the craft out of the air. The muffles
Which rifle an explosion
From a sphere
Into a linear discharge
On course for the boundless slightness.

He dreams of the ghost of intelligent behaviour, a shell which
Alters shape to keep its course. Three gyros on three axes
Describe the orientation of their platform: x, y, z. Cased off
From local influences, at the moment of exit they're looking for
Gravity which isn't there. He knows the place: a desert close to
The Equator. The time—close to dawn, the trackers can see the
Round in high contrast, as if slowed, out from co-axial

Streaks
           of fuel and
                        friction sparks.

Diffuse
           clarity
                        wiped over

A featureless,
           equable,
                        range.

The fluid substance of dawn draws its curve.
The human star races meteorites over the sand of Tyuratam.
A treader on emptiness, drinker of fire,
Whose eyes follow the sun and the moon.
Lightness razed a fletched titanium shell,
A tensed mouth caught the phonology of an explosion.
Rear the arch with no ground, scan the metre with no fall.
Where all the numbers of fire are bent from their vagrance
The slender spire ascends on heroic furies.

The lattice of snow and sunshine is thrown wide, the shatterer
Of forts unmasks his ordnance:
In the latitude whose sky flashes out of the arrow
The polisher of meteorites gazes through etched glass at cerebral fire.

The year is 1956. Korolev unlatches the sky.

In the nine lands of the Kolyma
An engineer is thrown down a mine shaft, the frozen ground
Refusing State corpses. Laid-by by the stere.
Was it all bluster? Impossibles
Left in from mere self-love, lyric nights
Scribbling wide figures? Some provincial genius
Laying out a new social system? The docket
Was never filed. The dying
Recite the names of the dead. Snowflakes
Fall to pick up a wink of heat
And draft up, vanishing in plain sight.

## Looks Like Luxury and Feels Like a Disease

He begs for a large view, he begs for needles.
He begs for a faceless coin, he begs for the heel of a loaf.

He begs not to be looked at. He begs
For a bag of mixed sweets, for wooden joints starting. He begs
For a holding of singles in shoeboxes, and for an Amstrad word
processor with a ZX81 chip.

He begs for a shirt from Camden Lock Market and a pair of old shoes.
He applies for countenance, aficionados and copycats.

He begs for a bag of apples and a bag of onions.
For a bus ticket to High Barnet and to win arguments.

He forages without shame.
Who now is our cause of laughter, who
Is faint when the bill arrives?
Who eats his own leavings?

He begs for milk and tea, or for fine yellow linen.
He begs for the scrapings of the pan,
And for long yards of red beer.

He solicits for the accord of prestige,
He begs for a shirt, and the holes in it.
He desires greasy victuals. He indents for
Formulae of release on sheets of lead.

He begs for silver foil as snug ticking.
He begs for a door-post when he sees it.
He picks more than he leaves.
He wants an ear for what knowledge he has.

He begs for place spiritual and temporal.
He begs a button for his coat.
He begs to be sick when he is well.
He begs for butter on hot lentils some times around.

He begs for an overcoat frayed at the cuff,
And for tears at the pockets and at the hem.
He begs for a passage of water looped
Under many tall blackthorn bushes.

He begs for a setting at the board, and to be privy to counsels.
He begs for expertise, and for a pleasing eagerness.
He likes his facts soft, his
Several sorts of data set out in one picture.

He wishes something for being nothing.
He tenders blank looks and the hollow of his hand.

Money for jam. Just the facts ma'am. Start me up. Pummel my lights,
Unfuddle my wits. A middle term plan. I'll be your man.
Two hands and a tongue. Fealty for sweets. More than a tease and less
Than a sneeze. Eight slices of brown bread. Many penny benefit.
Dosser stipendiary. Largesse of nobility. Decentred penalty.

Laid off solidary, don't take on so. Feet on the loose, heads
On the block. It's a big break, splurge these takings.
Self image no feature. Headstrong avenger.
Scavengeable loser. Illiquid vanguard.
Licenced for languor. What makes today's homes
So modern? the purely ornamental people.
No, Roseanna, we must wait for the sea to refill.
Cavitation bubble. Stuck to the pan. Pits in the metal.

Qualms at the till. No! to the frill. Part of your charm.
No-hope on a rope. Sloven up in arms.
Slip-ups from the trickledown. The say-sos of the so-said.
Slash to the bone. Stop at home. Artless Goth that nobody owns.
The counter staff sluice you through and out like droppings.
Get your intellectuals here, eight ounces a year. Cleaning
Duties included. Blank in a sweepstake, straw in a haystack.
Hay for wire and gorse for winter. No gain,
No pain. Great feckless Midlands lump.
Mouse soup in Flesh Hovel Lane. Pauper's traps, *de beaux draps*.
Put on your good clothes and write a poem. Gather fuel for an electric kettle.

*Pauper Estate* (1996-99)

Crusty old thing. Nowt for tat but lenience at that. A small fortune,
Chastity and thrift. Ditchwater on draught.
At the curt beck of the celestials we raise the Castle of Indolence.

In the Rawheel Café, where the claimants become clients,
The grate of the chicory in the coffee,
The thickness of the waitress's Kurdish accent,
Surpassed the merely generous and comforting.
Talk was cheap and geniality filled the stomach.

## Adesso non posso

The light rendering space erases and floods the brain
the sight of a noble torso and breast
luring something from its deep and dark sleep
to wake for a life of minutes.
A doorway through which a new self comes,
a room in which I came about.

A Sunday morning in 1963,
the screen on in the sitting room in our house in Loughborough,
I'm seven years old, a beautiful woman in a bedroom,
she starts to take her clothes off, smiles at someone,
her face is full of life, she moves gawkily but with nervy enthusiasm,
I gaze as if pouring myself into the picture, she is down
to a bodice of stiff black lace, and stockings,
my vein system rewiring itself while I watch
the black glamour object giving off blue heat, sheets
of new skin unwrapping themselves like white stars
opening in the tender sky of childhood. Suddenly her face changes,
she says
*No I can't*
*Not now*

A smell of something nameless and alive.
My body is soaked, new. The energy
stops at maximum, humming. A hand
picking me up by the hair, crushing and stretching me.
Reshown on my screen, incomplete, italiano
the scene shown in a lesson programme, Sunday morning's task,
I worked out as I learnt the grammar of the imaginary
it was Antonioni, the sudden girl with the long legs was Vitti. In 1991
I was queuing beside the Thames for 'La Notte', looking for that scene, for
the completion of the glimpsed, where
a woman too was turned back
whom I saw
sad, vague, excited,
crossing the café area of the concert hall next door, and caught up with,

*Pauper Estate* (1996-99)

And later
sketched a transformation scene
And later
completed the lesson
And later
conducted my life
through her gaze equipping frames
in which the desired experience is caught.
An improvisation of opposing actors,
a sift and indrift she searched for weighed patterns,
a polycentric replacing of scenes,
a dérive through places and institutions
—she shot her life as the last Antonioni film.
Nine days' queen or,
the decentralisation of the most privileged actions.
Superbly
              empty halls
                            we figure.
The women glamorous, the men alluring and disappointing,
this *mise en scène* she embraced
among the commands of the senseless
as modernity.
A space full of exactingly visible order,
geological masses emitting a Time whose recession
swallows us.
Woman who
       before seizing the lover
              writes the parting scene—
I was chosen
       for my lack of substance.

Scenes which after a thousand repetitions we repeat
quite impersonal, on whose lack our character founded;
unavoidably, in pure improvisation and loss of knowledge;
rhythmic, in scattered jags of folly and excess.
We part from desire to find the world disappeared.

Years later fumbling through the cabinet I realised
the type object may itself be a dealer's fine forgery

what we thought was the new lyric poetry
wasn't, on that TV screen in 1963
the one I saw tossing aside the secrets wrapping
a new power and a new chemical state
wasn't an Italian
it was you. A series outside time, recognition
searched out through a looping dark flame,
closed on me. Frames discarded like leaves around a candid core.

Bodiless self-imposing patterns, recursively sought after
where arousal and anxiety spiral and decline
as fixed sequences in the superflux, eject
a psychic anatomy. Vitti in black. Could I rewrite the scenes
I watched when I was thirteen, wandering round a town in Northamptonshire
with cropped hair? was It rehearsing the guilt of others towards me,
repeating gratification, dreams of being a writer? Rolled-up flats
in a huge old barn, waiting to be washed and fitted-up for the strolling
reverie. Roaming because trace minerals missing. Cellular hunger guides
a scanning spiral. The surface geometry of chemicals coded into a dream
            pattern.
In sleep I dive three miles deep, swimming through passible earth
to swipe at loose treasure. Calm ripples to the point of reflection. A room
            stacked with reels of cinema without the silver.
Light up the arc, and project a few frames. Eat
that dark, scarce, infinitely compacted light smeared on a stone wall.

Before waking I possessed you again,
a star tearing through my roof. Surfacing
through a heated lake
where I would have said,
Love, clutch these moments rushing of the night
catch this burst of heat, love,
fall as this scarlet hour falling

draws on shame terror repining.
Opulence and admiration sign inverted,
rage eye, vanishing point, projection source.
The day erased by 8 a.m., exhausted,
a round of idleness and vagueness.

*Pauper Estate* (1996-99)

1994. When I think
I get ill.
*Strip me down*
*Scavenge my parts.* I remember
to sign on.
Chastity, Diligence, Thrift: a new system
for a lyric poet.

A rich sensibility, a plane of ardent ideals,
where my exclusion is the entry of the aesthetic.
A fantasy relinking thousands of module scenes.
The consort of kitsch
concealing the adored anxious object
under a surface of powdered twirls.
*entre colchas de carmesí*

Between sheets of white hollands
And silk quilts of crimson
Maria Fernanda was singing.

*Pauper Estate* (1996-99)

## Least Energy Structures

Sealed compacted mud where heat is dead.
Full fall where way is none.
Flooded passageways and davits. Flush with resting bed. Plates gripped
    by balks of water.
Lading of sisal, tins of pineapple, coffee beans, sunflower seeds, ingot
    copper and zinc

Whose threads of decay off northwest Spain
beacon to the larvae of the worm *lamellibranchia*,
from untheorised crustal seeps under European waters,
where migrants carried phonetic structures;
they grid the sea, to grow internal Time where the
voice aqualandscape
is the foreknown place singing as drops on its skin.
*From passive drift acquiring new organs*

a lowest energy structure
of tiles with imaginary colours
liquid falls into the rules of geometry
a safe arrangement of my objects
the state of cooling where cooling can no longer occur
no adjacent space involves change
no symmetries to acquire flaws

*a lattice of vacancies and impurities*

Larval intelligence of one situation only
a ghost star-reckoning by nuzzling a trace
richness of the waters, rarefying as the cube of distance,
radio waves dissipating beyond the moon.
Travels at the surface where the light water spins,
diving when the contaminants say *here*
by an adjustment of internal pressure.

A body even in every direction
that cannot be split
imitating, never incorporating

*Pauper Estate* (1996-99)

Drawn by a lack,
I walk carefully in complete circles
guided by cellular want marking the skin of my face
 a self-repairing pattern
strained by the imperatives of symmetry

I chew the full organs of plants and animals,
proteins dismantling proteins with a knife of three-dimensional tiles.
Where membranes set a chemical break,
The I as a frequency curve, in a space of curves, a
lethality rule towards minor distributions,
a pattern that engorges other patterns,
an asymmetry in time which
pays itself back.
My rules
to filter spoil along a cascade of centrifuges
perspectively towards a climax
the one-way spiral, safe from recursions.

before phonemes. a border
where both sides are alike
and the boundless has the structure of a bed ooze.

*ash of apricot wood. ash of scenography. ash of a silk slip.*

## Least Energy Structures

Sealed compacted mud where heat is dead.
Full fall where way is none.
Flooded passageways and davits. Flush with resting bed. Plates gripped
      by balks of water.
Lading of sisal, tins of pineapple, coffee beans, sunflower seeds, ingot
      copper and zinc

Whose threads of decay off northwest Spain
beacon to the larvae of the worm *lamellibranchia*,
from untheorised crustal seeps under European waters,
where migrants carried phonetic structures;
they grid the sea, to grow internal Time where the
voice aqualandscape
is the foreknown place singing as drops on its skin.
*From passive drift acquiring new organs*

a lowest energy structure
of tiles with imaginary colours
liquid falls into the rules of geometry
a safe arrangement of my objects
the state of cooling where cooling can no longer occur
no adjacent space involves change
no symmetries to acquire flaws

*a lattice of vacancies and impurities*

Larval intelligence of one situation only
a ghost star-reckoning by nuzzling a trace
richness of the waters, rarefying as the cube of distance,
radio waves dissipating beyond the moon.
Travels at the surface where the light water spins,
diving when the contaminants say *here*
by an adjustment of internal pressure.

A body even in every direction
that cannot be split
imitating, never incorporating

Drawn by a lack,
I walk carefully in complete circles
guided by cellular want marking the skin of my face
 a self-repairing pattern
strained by the imperatives of symmetry

I chew the full organs of plants and animals,
proteins dismantling proteins with a knife of three-dimensional tiles.
Where membranes set a chemical break,
The I as a frequency curve, in a space of curves, a
lethality rule towards minor distributions,
a pattern that engorges other patterns,
an asymmetry in time which
pays itself back.
My rules
to filter spoil along a cascade of centrifuges
perspectivally towards a climax
the one-way spiral, safe from recursions.

before phonemes. a border
where both sides are alike
and the boundless has the structure of a bed ooze.

*ash of apricot wood. ash of scenography. ash of a silk slip.*

## Snow-puffed plumage

A Siberian wilderness turns, a thousand sleigh days on-end

to draw me into the space that has no danger
where gluts of energy vanished in their utterance
to a plane climax of effacement, that spaces out

monotony to nip in ideas their sonance
of hurt, stitching a night like toxic green stars;
sloping walls where each grain falls back and in.

Solitude takes the wanting out of want, love
sheathed in a blue heat signature, neutral, to
match the alien, in plump kilograms of old wool,

disuses this distending and narrowing in,
does not open on the rich, volatile, and piquant;
to live aimlessly and die obscurely.

## The Technique of Visualising

Raise both scene and characters
at blurred speed, in dazzling detail, with an internal past, with organic
	shading,
proper motion, in pinnacled steep recession
more consistent than truth, my heart knocking as
I embrace the dark lovely smoke, my veins
swollen with fumes. An intact cognitive line
surfaces on a pulse to raze what I recite and see,
cheating memory; the head which clears it made
from the same flesh as the error,
height in depth; at their juncture I grow dizzy and fall
and depth in height where reason wipes down to the grey shaking core.

Bleachprint.
No scene, no characters.
A carnal eye tracking on shifting ground.
This bliss, and terror durable as a jittering hand, I
added to the created world.

The big music of a hundred people working in exact
division of roles at highest strain, characters effaced and elevated.
A management graphic where I draw
a phased model of national revival and *roll'em Pete*.
Nets bright with fish. Stocks cleared at list price.
Messages pass, cut and winged, dripping unshared meanings.
A drama, a course to run, a colour or ambience
shaken out
a rapid succession of states
reshaping their human components and being reshaped.
A set of rules in every building,
botany of 700,000 firms as partite entries
in a Linnaean table kept in some State institute.
So many fish in transparent water
Swirling, no two following the same path,
Constrained by other paths. How to record

*Pauper Estate* (1996-99)

The whole? not seizing the line of local movement
Until the plan is there. Opening cold bright guts for their message,

Scooping out the narrative mud on the seabed, counting
The birds where they dive on churned water at the back of a wave.
Draw up a net full of fins and eyes.
Fitting a thousand pieces into a pattern, one piece
Into ten patterns.
There was a sludge in the pillars where an engineer
Sank a gauge telling the pressure on the bearing frame,
Checking the statics of a building holding 500 people,
System telltaled at a single point as if aware.
I open a hatch and the speed of a fluid tells me
How the *economy* is? The volatile luck sap
Bulging and overflowing in shop windows, trade ads, lorries rushing by.

I bear the epoch on my shoulders. No, in a shopping bag.

A door saying JOB CLUB above a white goods shop where
a small intense man tells us, there are 5 million people looking for work,
It's the 1840s, Marx knows the rules again, the bosses
have it just how they like and you've to be who they want.
A woman breaks down in sobs, he quietens her
Vision and fear of her fellow-citizens
Before telling us we can't resist him. Not on
Round about forty-five quid a week. Show me your CV.
At two choices, of taking his group to the streets
And storming the government seat of Barnet, or foretelling
Victory through subservience, he shouts at shared doubt
As if trying to boil a pond by body heat. Tie
Yourself in knots and we'll
Pay for the string.

*Pauper Estate* (1996-99)

## Precipice of Niches

1,
The latest wish of
a data fish
that eats and becomes an ego
that swallows and is hungry again

a mineral ego
grinding the beds of earth for pigments
of grey and blue
soaking into the colours of the landscape
growing faint at the burial of rays
the curve where its mouth closes
dispersing over the bed of the visible
to swallow itself at the horizon line

soft as an eye and fresh as air
the droppy deity of sweet water
that falls everywhere
and uses the sky as its path

naked in flash floods
a niche fish that knows in flashes
that adopts the colour of the air
and recites the tale as told it

the casing of volatile sound

a niche fish flushed with signs
that worships the living waters above the dead


2,
The coast was called Moors in Hell
its rocks lurched in twisted planes
where a cliff had slipped its step and top-
pled, split and split again

to become the seabed;
ruin as complexity, interior swallowing each surface,
riddled, a perfect refuge for what hides
and haunt for what catches
a geometry of fine-scale degradation
in its traps and part-worlds

The viewing-glass viewed
the pored littoral paradise
scattered over many acres,
in frames, in niches
its bursts and splashes of rock,
surfaces glinting red green and tawny
scored with blind signs, gripped by shells,
each pit fitting
the strange anatomies of the deep

3,
*The eye that sheds grains of dust*

The hypothesis
of the X-wind
the flux double-peak, the X-zone
where a star's metals splash out & escape
like water that leaves the sea,
and a flake away where a lash of the Sun's magnetic field,
moving in, slung matter out from its outer edge
spume dense enough to aggregate
on an orbit where growth & cooling were possible:
the spores of a planet

The tidemark
a phase trapped in chondrule insets, in
falls of Libya and Antarctica
meteorite eye protected by stone
whose ball retains the archaeology of a vapour
aluminium isotopes marking a boiling point,
heavy nuclei a solar origin

slender birth line of a planet
solution to a kinetic geometry
marginal to so many dead states
slowed on a slope of dispersal & destruction
becomes its own environment, an I-scene
cascade of self-speeding attractiveness
trapping indifferent volleys of impacts

the twin of dead twins
of isotopes vaporizing into derelict wastes,
that uniquely peaks with the recurring turning-back,
the self-storing spores


4,
A passive and incomprehensible surface
a culture leaving its Time in puzzles and masks
wonderful & unfamiliar self, a perfect refuge
growing and dividing at visible speed
tremulous in many leaves dancing,
in vaults where the deep dark forms sift and sop around
recreating shells of lost moments
where horizons part and deny each other
a foam of local ends to vision
a matrix shimmering with traps and part-worlds

Short-lived selves discolouring in a decay cycle
a shell of evanescent subsonic waves
in the field recordings of ritual music
the square scripts of the southern oases
recording the high death of ibexes
solution to a kinetic geometry
for the replenishment of the high springs
eyes of water where unknown wishes surface

as we swallow the rich and alien forms
a fan of dialects & early inscriptions falling
down a slope of broken symmetries
we ascend to match the past

spreading in a strained and saturated web
sets dense in doubles & contrasts form
a screen allowing us to ignore all sounds

passing into temporary bodies
linked to capes of sensation
craving for rare metals, the slopes of old
rock stiff with solar riches
pursuing the slender birth line of birds
to the Western shores
wings sheathed in the fossil matrix
a complex made serial
and anatomy formed in myth
recurring time
where the darkness opens its eyes to us
its rare phonemes & brilliant plant dyes

## Andy-the-German Servant of Two Masters

The right family connections
and an edited biography. Deep cover
and a foreseen shortage of infantry wars. Theorist
of stalking. Long-range shooting
is mainly
a *spiritual* thing

The first thing you do, you get them
to buy automatic weapons
This breaks the ice and makes their fingers tingle.
One hand on the bottle and one...

Andy, Mr *Bundesverfassungsschutz* is not Budweiser,
Talked as much as someone with a mouthful of water.
That is, he swallowed the words and passed the water out as social gifts
How much can a building really take?

Ritsch, ratsch
hang out the trash. The jury will buy
a limited hang-out. America for the Americans
Shine for the shoeshine boys
Land for the lords. Sacks for the shucks.
Elohim City for Oklahoma.
Draff for the hogs. Fish for the seals.
A bag for the sleaze. A bowl for the dust.

Time for crime. Day for night. Green for red.
Beyond the beaming tautologies, everything
profound loves a mask, and
people with dirty souls
don't wear swoop necklines.
The ATF guys weren't in the office that day
the office blew out of the building
Blew the town. No-showed their showdown.
Blow the gaff. Cut the smoke
in the open-plan with its façade cut away
to foreclose the government. Blow it out your ears.

Ozarks-scale gene pool bi-bi-bitten by a gun bug
Doorstep Andy selling a script
like throwing sticks for a dog.

Way down
way over where the steel rods breach
where the steel pins break-dance
where the parked cookup cracks the theorised linear frame,
watch out! where the classic curve of a blast wave
met the tectonic cement cubes
at the imaginary point in geometry;
and a citizen's rights man
with a doctorate in the mathematic of ruin,
brass Air Force general with
big back-up in negative civil engineering says
no way
could McVeigh have torn their playhouse down
We control the horizontal
He heard a skip-beat in the wall of sound

we control the vertical.
The updating of moral consensus. The conduct
of the gaze. Altering shared ideas
by cover of night. Sending to fantasies.
Threads run out as clues
adding grey noise to data excess
in a screen with key escrow. Where sight lines converge,
pinned against the horizon, a thief sideways
behind your back. How come the musicians know
what's coming next? From shoo-in to death-watch,
spinning data back through a false third party.
Hiding pattern in pattern, breaking outlines,
snap-point shear from appliquéd charges on the pillars.

I'm gonna run to the City of Refuge,
turn about, hire a captain of the watch
with the skills of a career infantry officer,
crossing the Great Plains without breaking a contour line.
The oculist of blind spots just walked in through the in door.

Fully automatics for the camp guards.
Elohim City Compound
is the outside of the inside.

Andy two for one. Andy fluent in the manly skills,
draw them in over the head handy.
The barrels are beautifully rifled and the marksmen
are destabilised, we figure
someone who believes what we believe
is too double dumb to double talk
a trick track where the phase of confined movement
flows on from conducted freedom of action.

Blow, Illinois, blow! the righteous highs
of homesteader holdouts, Indian killers
and Bible readers, stake racers
and redneck heads of household;
their gold,
        guns
                and water
clinking on taut skin, tall-walkers
waving half a wit taught
civics by an
occupation government. Up-country
applejack and freeze-dried buffalo cocks.
Plenty too smart to eat soil.
Keepsakes from the Dolly Parton Theme Park,
Theologoumena in No Roads County.

A fervour of conjecture
where whatever fleshes out the fixed idea
is drawn in to draw on,
bent surface proteins as wrappers for
the end of the game. It was like selling
perimeter captains to paranoids.

While the verses give no light, living out of
the back of a truck, running with
a travelling gun fair, the country

flaring behind you like a contrail, from mesas
to trailer parks, wrapped up tight at
the vanishing point. The round jumps straight
and for a moment
your soul is held between your shoulder and forefinger.
The pamphlets go out with the home defense goods.
Sight line, white lines,
riding the hiss-hot rails to a place of Federal care.

Antelope headgear of a mimic
spear-carrier.
A verbal trail discarded by
military intelligence is
interference pattern:
leopard's spots against
tree foliage
blinking with sun.
Antique stalker skills bagging
a far political organisation.

One hand on the bottle and one…
Andy sitting out at night with a Midwest blonde.
Andy's square-dancing drill squad pissing testosterone
slapping heel and toe with the Hessian.
Steadily losing arguments with the Devil.
Rolling in the Surrey with the fringe on top
Andy knocking in stakes and lines in Strassmeir County,
buying federally restricted rounds by FedEx.
Andy kickin' back. Andy digging Western Swing.
Andy fading up the patches of blur.
A lurk in the lurch. Damned straight, in the straddle.

# 'From Zenith to Pupil': a Northern Summer

fleeting actinic magentas

the smallest rim of a night you
could catch in your hand and
hang upon a tree

sheets of soluble purples
phantoms in gold leaf
staring serried in a dandelion halo of blur
thin air-basking in the unslanting unquenched
they watch to replete themselves with rarety
the mill of beams
its Hyperborean candour
a subtle gush of serotonin
pure Time, the draught of winning speed.
A deflector to cup the core as it shatters—

a trajectory
copied by the warriors in bird masks
brains soaked in living light
drawn along the meridian
like a crane along its flight:
a ray from a small soundless star

stress breaks into sound, a hai!
a universe of knowledge, before the
eye for only the frail
anatomy of a moment,
developed
by flourishes of straight and oblique lines,
bursts and scatters, a new plane joins itself up

the light sighs and shifts in quality

# Weapons Form with Music, #18

After three days' travel through the lands burnt by the English
at dawn they reached the beach by Castle Sween
where Himself was in residence, at oversight
of the vintage—dense ranks of ancient wine-presses
driven by spiral iron shafts with grapes as knobs
crushing the gush out of thick, ripe, splashing, purple bunches
which wooden tuns with yard-wide grins could hardly swallow
while the malting of Sweeney's barley
covered the sea with warm and sprightly fumes

And the gallowglass prince entertained them
in his snug hall entirely of red yew boards
frequently reciting from a vellum script in silver ink
tales called *Cogadh Suibhne,*
*The Ranter's Foray, Sweeny furioso,*
*Strange Tales of Barry at the White Tiger Studio,*
*Outstanding Quagmire Tactics of the Redshanks,*
and *Metrical Errors of Blind Arthur MacGurkich.*

A bit of an old Celtic relic
limestone foundations worn by sea-salt
but wearing his face with pride
that long handsome gentle dandy.

Fire and glass, in ample supply,
stripped the barley brew of its dark husks,
there dripped in overlapping furls
a pale supple rainlike run of strength

And so the heroes rested.

*Savage Survivals* (1999-2005)

## The Ruins of Guldursun

To start with the fading. The animation
in its virtual planes shedding cells, washing back;
the wind sand which is all pictures and none;
a beach of coloured grains where acuity slides away.
Just a desert, and the word *kanat*.
The parting sand rising into conjecture,
the void ground packing the propylaeon maze.
A difference of culture on microscopic scale, or
from mould ferment to abrasion
in the small porosity of the mesh your water slips
distilled in plain sight away from, the lexical gaps
between smoke and dust?
To proceed with the lighting. *dar zamin dur dast*
The shimmering surface of ignorance plying itself
where eye and hand make place, and sweeping
what they gain into what they lose: dullness
mimes, and blurs, the swimmer's shape,
somnolence swallowing what its surface copies
in lump darkness feathering at the edge.
Twisting itself out of vacancy in a thin air, the castle
*aust i korusm*, to the east of the Aral Sea,
the set of sounds at modest cost in the cellar,
the guardian tenuity
past which the focus of the drifter flares and flicks on
through the developed and exploded spaces
quite small in this labyrinthine shining.
The roof covered with apricots, parching.
Following heuristic loops, in 1936, Tolstov;
good German glass all found, and comforted by tea.
Concentric, circular, named: Guldursun,
blind spots all swept, its layout dualist.
A set of winds furling,
the fine development that vanishes as we go through it,
floss metal radiating to its own tenuousness.
A lost word and the array of all words
amounting to the same account:
a shower of mica and a stitch of water.

Where the strength of the sun slopes, and the starlight
is cold enough to walk upon,
Zoroaster, in the belts of falling white, turning and
framing sets of law and turning; the son
of rainwater that fell on thirsty grass. A copy
learnt and carried by each of a million,
from among the thick splashes of speech,
disposing the city in the order in which sounds arrive,
before the city was built.
The brewing of tea from ephedrine, and the course
of Nine Words of Power
which raise dead clay, make its limbs
listen to its head, its head listen to a shared array,
its skin grow firm and red, about a paired order; genial,
picking out a neurological tune;
the individual consciousness or organ of faith
set about with swept eyes and with timed commands.
The tea makes his ears glow and muscles tighten.
And he did listen
and that sound that was blind
separated itself
over the Thraco-Cimmerian plains with the white heads of cotton,
Iranian tongue denied to something more elusive, sinistral,
and the eyeless disquieting roar
shone with the floods of light slashing through it
over a course of horse pastures where /s/ turns to /k/
the lost phonology in its cube of oral geometry,
on the banks of the ancient workings of water
west of Tokharian, north perhaps
of Scythian. The currency flow led across the detaining web
in the hours the water master allotted,
in numbered surges at the raising of a slat or hatch
softens the syllabic peaks of sound, the air column
detailed by onsets and lapses.
To complete with the flakes of pigment.
The Tiger and Pheasant Chamber,
charming in red and blue, the rolls of moist forest
coveted by the court, patches fallen from the wall,
for delicate hours; a second shape crossing
where deep rips run on and off the brilliance.

*The Imaginary in Geometry* (1999-2003)

## The Spirit Mover, 1854
*(Spirits instructed Roger Spear to make a machine)*

The neural telescope, the chalk writing
in his brain, the On High's make order.
Vortexes forming words. A cosmic plughole
drains. Barriers thin on the cliff at Lynn
in cracked air. Revd. Spear rapt, a call centre.
missing music or, for example, a Cody novelette,
bodiless words chalking out a machine design
two thousand dollars of piece parts at High Rock cottage.

Up with the nineteenth. The spirit world modernising
reads knowledge in the eyes of the dead.
Way past the Bourbons. Laughs at the Romanovs.
Envious of the Hapsburgs' railway concessions.
Techno sylph's trance downloads franchised, Speared,
construction loyally done without analytical overlay.
Yankee spirits with barns, abounding good sense.
Electric ships, circular cities shipped as kits
technical details delivered in 200 updates
a kind of *waffling* of brass and copper.

The four winds' cymbal under the roof of trance. Slender
antennae spiring to where ideas come from
driven by words or weather.
Fin flash. Crash barrier. Revd. Spear lashed, in a bell of
'metal plates, strips, and gemstones', diver,
bad vibrations damped, hauls up to the Mover.
It is a new age *a stream of light from his body*
The device of unknown purpose—the spirits' Model T—
starts in to tremble.

Small thrills of bells and copper rods. Hairs rare.
The nerves unsteady for hearing the ghostly
falling to the surface of the earth
like pennies to the bottom of the sea.
Small fossil of an electricized future. Fine turns,

the making visible of a self-stating vortex
winding on. The Mover pauses its paces, sits out,
splutters, can't find a groove. No ding or tinkle.
Some spirits deceive. Some don't grasp engineering principles.
High times in Cattaraugus County
*that lofty electrical position*
Inside a rage machine, the good people of the parish
riled up to a storm, earthing a force,
they shout the same words, smash.
The Mover
disaggregates into zinc and brass
the shell working in a new mode as modules trip out.
Spirits rescued, forked crackles, blue parachute. Bale-out.
Gulp cobalt. Up and away. From the disassembly.

## Q-landscapes

Imagine a cherry if it were missing
restore its redness;
entire social orders unlatched & dropped into forgetting

Flushed bright faces of the women,
deferential pride of the sheep
a rosy-cheeked firm-skinned manly jawed resolution
or, expression no. 9
of the hero who only appears in photos.

Kew, interviewed
in an Albany flat
full of calfskin bindings and sports kit:
"The shape of my face changes every Spring
I used to work as St Michael in a cathedral
carved and stained red, green, and gilt
trampling a stock, mottled devil with teats,
lapped in a starry cloak of shaved linenfold oak.
I've spent fruitful years as an inn-sign,
or in a naval melodrama with tableaux,
tars hauling at the trunnions of a six-pounder,
myself declaiming bravely in blue,
shoulders swagged with Chatham bullion,
stiff enough to brace
a silly plot"

*How does it feel to be just a projection?*
I only start to exist when the lights go on.
Otherwise I just rest or try on hats

Flicking gloves like fans, Crispian Kew
attends a Bond Street shop, his exquisite sensations
flowing round the commodity system,
a ripened life we contact through objects,
fetched by the salesman who
sheds a tear of joy

at seeing the negligent eye that retains everything.
He pays in mint sovereigns,
turns to reveal that his head has no back;
an affluent shimmer, a legend. a quality of light.

A candid mime
of the young, brilliant engineer
astray in the higher symbolism
while crashing his bicycle
feeling the breakpoints on his fingertips
in his spiky scrawled test log—the new wonder textile.
The mill is saved! the tennis shirt is reinvented!

Cantabrian oak cargo
of young barrels rolled through the miles of cellar
behind the wharf, vault ceilings softened
with lacy fungus living on fumes of wine
clever metabolic mouth
in grape sugar ripples
whose skin is its wings
casks swollen tight with catacomb moisture
languid connoisseur drawling in dark beamy rooms
where Kew drinks and, significantly, says nothing.

Caught in seven seconds catching
a perfectly casual quip replayed at will
reframing a recurred concern.
Emphasis on faces defining space—
good looks giving off assurance in fruity waves
—as anxious as a pack of hounds all running one way
the colour of a room that lets us enjoy
the exclusion of the disenchanted
Security fastened by advances in the depth of field
breaking down movements to release the steady and requited—
an odour of saddle-soap and expensive cologne

Sociably, sociably
they set out in the faint light of dawn
to reach the peak and recover the plain

*The Imaginary in Geometry* (1999-2003)

for whom the snowy beinn is as a tiepin
striking off a tie; for whose sake
the whole landscape breaks up and shakes itself out
thousands of tons and soil pivoting weightlessly,
greens eagerly becoming greener, pondwater becoming bright
to complement this plenary pose against it

After gazing at the champions of wit and generosity
you buy their clothes and trappings,
Like oil like feathers the Jermyn facings
the fell of a royal animal, quality
like a spirit-glass fuming in a cone
draped in lengths of fitted & gored cloth
flaring like fire in a pine
in light inaccessible
hid from the eye

Kew affable but never uttering,
charmingly less intelligent than his overcoat
in the flawless Q landscape
supporting a paper cut-out of a gent;
it asks the company to acknowledge
sex wealth and stability
but not too much

The svelte and swift in Apollinary games
to solve the question of time
the perfection of the arbitrary
*white flanks and mulberry tree*
The shimmering everywhere of collusion
a thousand little touches signalling
the presence in themselves of what they admire
negligent
repeatable
discreet

Rejoice in the Modern Style villa in Richmond
rejoice in Edmund, king of East Anglia
rejoice in the birds of the sea of Deucalydon

rejoice in the bashful yielding of the sloe to gin
rejoice in the engraved papers in their boxes at Coutts'
rejoice in his money out on the Baltic Exchange
rejoice in his failure to achieve solidity

## On the Beach at Aberystwyth

The ocean stops where I stand,
the beach cuts it off with a gesture. On the hill
the grumbling old men
hadn't written the books I wanted, leaving me
loose on a beach lapping out of sight
in a spin too slow to be at a loss, to
fetch from underfoot what lost footing,
a stock lump called *babalwbi*,
Silurian drift of air wafer like the surf
turning lateral sibilants into chain alliteration,
*fossilised coral*
fallen from the sea full of the likes of us
the boats the sheep, the
words you soften at the start and slenderize at the end.
Space built up of passages that interconnect
but never go far, could we use that
for a littoral chain-stitch
not rich in roads and towns
where what stops in Skye
might start in Marrakesh? the maths
of an endless surface and no outside
that could reckon
not the ocean
checkless moving around one fluid northwest axis
but the concept of the ocean
the very wash of our geosophy
emergent glass with 360 panes and no centre.
Facing headway through the Celtic archipelago
a boundless littoral
unrolled like linen
where you are never any further away.
The mirror washing in shears twin planes of social laws
of phoneme arrays
Spanish town names matched to Irish ones
shimmering steam of beached wave drafting curves.
A cassocked figure leans from the pier

and shouts down
distinctly, but in Welsh,
*Where are you from?*
*What is social structure?*
*How is experience organised?*
*What are the rules which permit you to identify?*
*Beth ydy adeiladwaith cymdeithasol?*
On a bank of this sea province
how we think of it is our choice
as a set of excellences recorded in strict verse
a line of hops between soft coves for coastal vessels
the movement of formal groups conducted by sound,
the running of beef and hides down to arid Spain,
or a set of symbolic objects tied to real ones
for the purpose of exchange;
the way we go is what we find
a non-scalar map of references
pointing out from either side of my head
where my senses lie collecting:
suspend now the eastern seaboard and the French investment,
hang on to Tartessus
the monopole of the whole pastoral recession:
bales with red stamps in Punic business hand:
at St Malo
heathland grains, buckwheat made up into pancakes
the prevalence of cats by the fishermen's dock:
out on the Western Approaches
waiting for the clouds to part
and show the conduct of the stars:
standing off from a Cornish promontory
the Cyclopean villages visible inland
stone jambs where timber is an import
the sheltered gully, green, down
to a porth with the fishing smacks drawn up:
at the mouth of the Ystwyth
wading through the surf shouting about a hot drink
falling along the predrawn lines of least distance.
Or, how was Spain before the Spaniards
whether Pokorny was right about those Berber cattle breeds

*The Imaginary in Geometry* (1999-2003)

or come to that the Iberian verb system,
an eager sort of Bronze Age dog,
or a kind of sheep used to travelling by boat.

a 3-dimensional meander
salt flake glistening
in curved inlet
drawn lax vacuity
bringing forth wealth
inmost healing loss

detritus whose environment is itself                    [the CORAL
wafer fluency
a skeletal tendril
pitted with permeations
backwash drifts
cellular vortex
recessively lapped

How much of the Atlantic
in each pore of coral? how much
of the oceanic culture strain
secured in me?
A scale pattern
of a living sense dissolving at a glance.
Jitter to hold the jitter thing holding me
my eye failing for want of cleats
on a skittering fishscale surface
lost, a dust of clattering sounds
in the topos of egoless states
seized in a net and unseized.
You just latch one patch of behaviour onto another
fetched out from an open boat
onto an open shore
breeding to comfort the sheep.
One hill is not a failed copy of the next in range,
the vacancies are made of individuals
but not clarified as posts,
social that *same old riddle*

and shouts down
distinctly, but in Welsh,
*Where are you from?*
*What is social structure?*
*How is experience organised?*
*What are the rules which permit you to identify?*
*Beth ydy adeiladwaith cymdeithasol?*
On a bank of this sea province
how we think of it is our choice
as a set of excellences recorded in strict verse
a line of hops between soft coves for coastal vessels
the movement of formal groups conducted by sound,
the running of beef and hides down to arid Spain,
or a set of symbolic objects tied to real ones
for the purpose of exchange;
the way we go is what we find
a non-scalar map of references
pointing out from either side of my head
where my senses lie collecting:
suspend now the eastern seaboard and the French investment,
hang on to Tartessus
the monopole of the whole pastoral recession:
bales with red stamps in Punic business hand:
at St Malo
heathland grains, buckwheat made up into pancakes
the prevalence of cats by the fishermen's dock:
out on the Western Approaches
waiting for the clouds to part
and show the conduct of the stars:
standing off from a Cornish promontory
the Cyclopean villages visible inland
stone jambs where timber is an import
the sheltered gully, green, down
to a porth with the fishing smacks drawn up:
at the mouth of the Ystwyth
wading through the surf shouting about a hot drink
falling along the predrawn lines of least distance.
Or, how was Spain before the Spaniards
whether Pokorny was right about those Berber cattle breeds

or come to that the Iberian verb system,
an eager sort of Bronze Age dog,
or a kind of sheep used to travelling by boat.

a 3-dimensional meander
salt flake glistening
in curved inlet
drawn lax vacuity
bringing forth wealth
inmost healing loss

detritus whose environment is itself                    [the CORAL
wafer fluency
a skeletal tendril
pitted with permeations
backwash drifts
cellular vortex
recessively lapped

How much of the Atlantic
in each pore of coral? how much
of the oceanic culture strain
secured in me?
A scale pattern
of a living sense dissolving at a glance.
Jitter to hold the jitter thing holding me
my eye failing for want of cleats
on a skittering fishscale surface
lost, a dust of clattering sounds
in the topos of egoless states
seized in a net and unseized.
You just latch one patch of behaviour onto another
fetched out from an open boat
onto an open shore
breeding to comfort the sheep.
One hill is not a failed copy of the next in range,
the vacancies are made of individuals
but not clarified as posts,
social that *same old riddle*

*always starts in the middle* structure
where language flows through foramina
and runs in suspended circles
gently expanding
to amount to a family.
But what I think *is* where I live
by the estuary calmly funnelling craft
from the outcomes of the Parisian Basin
and its weatherproof hangars of goods and ideas
for an hour each side of high tide.
Out here, populations don't aggregate
they carry poems in their head
packed in rules of assonance
a kind of enforced surplus of symmetry—
(this crossed the water sometime)—
memorising the faces of hundreds of sheep
consulting the neighbours and people like that
linguistic waves, slowing towards the western baffle,
deflecting off the Alps with whole holes.
(What's this? ethnicity as *mispronunciations*?
the borders as
awkward lumps in the sound cone?)
Poetry in the absence of cities
fused with kindreds
as the superindividual might.

The horizon draws knowledge into a curved line
from facts into grammar
a board
within which space has callable rules
of transit & contingency & locale.
The shingle addresses the whole question of proximity
turning over and over
too small-cut to possess memory,
the smoothness of outward records contact time.
The ocean uses fishes to weigh down its catch of water,
uses pebbles to count its pebbles.
I seize on the brilliant stones
and to ruffle the surface of loss

*The Imaginary in Geometry* (1999-2003)

throw them away again—
she threw me back into the ocean
at St Ives or nearby
and I swam with the fishes
cruising the domain of the soluble
with a lot of tender moistening and re-surfacing
and like a little bit of Avonian driftwood
I bob into shore here in Aberbabalwbi,
like a gull skittering over a slate roof the
loss skittering over the sea, and The Matters keeping
in the National Library up on the hill—
I head back to the values of ice-cream and sunshine.
A little light rain
to bring the ocean to a scale we can handle,
as a wash of loving forgiveness.
I am what I think,
the culture *is* what it says
the ocean starts where it *ends*

## Abundance

Mood pulses in actinic glare
Wegener's three-colour system
three vertices of a catching frame

Light swooping through frissons of ice
thaws the coloured pane and freezes
the summer pastures of Greenland

The North Atlantic rush of a feathered turbine
swooping onto timed abundances
the flickering upwelling feast
the balmy fat-smeared surfaces
rattle of wing-racks

Shore to which they soar in summer skeins
fatal beyond Faeroe

Humus too poor for thorps and acres
incorruptible in the dusk of declension
The wrong island
the effect of latitude on group size

Scant askance slats of sunshine
slight aslant tints
skimming the captor mesh
grudging

Instrument scales on the objectless plane of light
notches against ice-blink
straining of sight on white
unscattered clarity where distance is near
trueness where farness is too sheer
scaleless blank plane
the eye flat falling without eyefast
from Lewis to the last land

Wisps of heat dissipation
drafting crystal austere polygons
starring of sea-ice from petalled edges
feathers flicking thermal flakes

## When Myth Becomes History


Breaking
the rim linking the story back to itself
A pipe broken with Time flowing out of it
the arrival of character
the onset of calculation
Marble eaten by a fungus which takes its shape
Stone wings defiled by a web of pink blood
sound breaking up into words
Cheap prophets with rhyming oracles
from hymn to annal

The spattered windrows of the stars foretelling
the lairs of metals lagged in the earth
fall silent. From god-tale to chronicle
the divine responses set out as law-code
shimmering on the mouths of the courts, distracted into paradox

The count of limbs fixed
the son looking like the father
The birds who forget the language of men
The hills stop in their place
and the property boundaries are drawn to each other

The rain of objects full of niches,
their features made of damage,
worked by adze, a speaking blade

A candid and sure-footed sound
so rich in partitions and symmetries
a group identity pouring over us without flowing away
a symbol that whirls the building around its head

hexagonal black temple of the tardy god
Calendar rites of reparative time
bathing in warm water with tamarisk, wax, pine-cones, oil and sugar
baraka transmitted from the dead

dish of flour saffron spikenard cloves & oil
the brain mimetic of star energies
the pattern lashed with interference shadows
breaking up at cellular level
a huff from the shaggy muzzle of a musk ox


## 2/ On the Margins of Great Civilisations

She sews what her mother sewed
the figures left from another age
disposed with the frontality of Parthian art
the ceremonial scene locked
signed with its objects
new linen sufficient for a descent.
Attached with the tall hat or *mitra*, the *akinakes*—
it is Respendial, king of the Alans. It is Caspar of the Ardagarantes.
The royal insignia in likeness sufficient
for a lost observer. An embroidered towel
for peasant prestige, for the glory of huts,
scutched stalks of linen, tinted with bright plants

In the margins of the great empires
provincial cultures turning slowly on themselves
a self-locking aggregate crossing the rim
of recurring. The abiding, the filling. Tales
in the prison where Campanella was held

Occluded
at the place where nothing is altered, the bottom
of a great lake
Let us enter the greater forgetting
far from the decay of forms
mere laggards in the march of high ideas
disposed in the likeness of goodness
descend in the likeness of companionship

In the fertile meadows, with the water-furrows
sacred objects of clay and bog-timber

## When Myth Becomes History

Breaking
the rim linking the story back to itself
A pipe broken with Time flowing out of it
the arrival of character
the onset of calculation
Marble eaten by a fungus which takes its shape
Stone wings defiled by a web of pink blood
sound breaking up into words
Cheap prophets with rhyming oracles
from hymn to annal

The spattered windrows of the stars foretelling
the lairs of metals lagged in the earth
fall silent. From god-tale to chronicle
the divine responses set out as law-code
shimmering on the mouths of the courts, distracted into paradox

The count of limbs fixed
the son looking like the father
The birds who forget the language of men
The hills stop in their place
and the property boundaries are drawn to each other

The rain of objects full of niches,
their features made of damage,
worked by adze, a speaking blade

A candid and sure-footed sound
so rich in partitions and symmetries
a group identity pouring over us without flowing away
a symbol that whirls the building around its head

hexagonal black temple of the tardy god
Calendar rites of reparative time
bathing in warm water with tamarisk, wax, pine-cones, oil and sugar
baraka transmitted from the dead

*The Imaginary in Geometry* (1999-2003)

dish of flour saffron spikenard cloves & oil
the brain mimetic of star energies
the pattern lashed with interference shadows
breaking up at cellular level
a huff from the shaggy muzzle of a musk ox


### 2/ On the Margins of Great Civilisations

She sews what her mother sewed
the figures left from another age
disposed with the frontality of Parthian art
the ceremonial scene locked
signed with its objects
new linen sufficient for a descent.
Attached with the tall hat or *mitra*, the *akinakes*—
it is Respendial, king of the Alans. It is Caspar of the Ardagarantes.
The royal insignia in likeness sufficient
for a lost observer. An embroidered towel
for peasant prestige, for the glory of huts,
scutched stalks of linen, tinted with bright plants

In the margins of the great empires
provincial cultures turning slowly on themselves
a self-locking aggregate crossing the rim
of recurring. The abiding, the filling. Tales
in the prison where Campanella was held

Occluded
at the place where nothing is altered, the bottom
of a great lake
Let us enter the greater forgetting
far from the decay of forms
mere laggards in the march of high ideas
disposed in the likeness of goodness
descend in the likeness of companionship

In the fertile meadows, with the water-furrows
sacred objects of clay and bog-timber

the beer takes on the likeness of the birchwood bowl
*outworn relics of ethnic migrations*
Only what starts from zero is a game
only what is renewable is melody


### 3/ Anagoge, or, When History Becomes Myth

Posed for the photographer
a reality that looks like the ideal
all gun barrels and hot black eyes
gazing steadfastly back, on the Campanian crag
paladin of regional apocalyptic lore
the brigand Luciana sewed up in leather pants
in apron, with folded cloth draped on head and neck
Mauser rifle and a brace of Belgian pistols for balance
wooden shoes and silver rowels
living on medlars, small birds, and chickpeas
a complete assemblage tilting the frame into myth

Swept away by the transformation scene
flesh all turned to wings
Luciana in linen
riding along the river Derwent on a winter afternoon
at one with rocks and water, drawing the sun down,
ibis and starfish sewn on her shirt. A broad-brimmed hat.
Fulfilling the star cults of personal salvation;
the shining track, the elliptical ridings;
the sky catalogues on the charts at Gospel Oak.
Stars plucked from the tree that lattices the sun.

## Silver Threads and Golden Needles
*the history of commercial capital*

Filaments for the bodying of an angel
the Flanders work of shaded gold
we see the unseen,
nimbus radially flaming on a cope in high relief.

This is *my* public vision
*my* soul and public knowledge narrating each other
don't interrupt me till I reach the end.
From Lydia and the first coinage of metal to make price serial,
to the Gotlandish Shore and the Grote Kraweel
I patched together the whole bin of shots
my eye devouring objects as if
they would not change and defect.

*Derelict parts of experience*
*held by fine stitches*
I saw world history and the struggle of classes
a sweep
from the sacral way at Pergamon
to the display windows of Bond Street shops
that was building visions and rolling them
inside a tube of sheer steel walls
showing the spirit in the mass
a mighty current whirling on a cloud of fragments
emphasizing lines that fall serenely and certainly
where every part is spoken by its own demon
driving shafts through a solid structure
where every cell has its share of information.

*Those containing noble metals are sold in three qualities*
*by troy weight, the Admiralty or Government standard at 1/90*
*the normal quality called gold 1/50*
*and the cheaper called gilt, taking discolouration in time*

I write a tune the actors can't hear,
part of my brain twirling in an airy motion
that doesn't shake light objects.
This is the tin of splicing cement
this is the throw of projection.
The blade that met the editing marks
flashes to fasten and to warn,
the same shots fit together more than one way,
rowed to sustain and falsify
the clear valley that abounds for the wide eye,
offered and receding.

A flickering screen
a fitting that amplifies and tilts and shutters.
Inner truth a colour flux, a splash of
light dying in the silver salts of film
sinking to couch itself in pigmented waves.

*Coloured threads clouding gold ones*
*chatoyant luminous and bodiless*
*the non-human flying clouded in human texture.*
*The form of angels made the space visible*
*but we could not enter in.*

## Trust

Climbing upwards through a tube of light
to an opening
where the question is how to spend one's life.
A camera bursting through doors into the back office
where brilliant intellects at work on the Mitigator Project
are moving round each other at improbable speeds
to take the country's care and keep its sake.
Crackling crisscross talk,
faces whose muscles are disposed
to unlock a trust we weren't keeping for later

Moments of suspension where
the switches of rage are switched
from heart to mind
the culture cultivating
as a pattern in time
decentralised and my own

Knotting and swallowing the wish
to follow at heel in the hope of becoming such a person
and be held up on the kind unsteady hands
eighty feet in the air
always falling, always caught
my heart turning over & my heart turning over

Trust in the colour of faces
trust in the Oxford accent
trust in strong tea and persistent puzzling
trust in the groundwater of sexual energies
Trust forms, concretises, attaches, grows warm,
projects, over-extends, is falsified, falls away,
forms, stops moving, attaches to a surface,
flies around,
projects a 3D pattern, goes too far, quarrels,
is ripped away, flies on, flips over, sinks out,
lands, solidifies, attaches to a bare skin, grows warm,

warms the eye, warms a pattern, finds flaws,
falls away, is ripped up, takes off, is detached,
acquires distance, is wrenched with longing,
flies around, grows eyes, searches,
gets lucky, gets married, carves an object

The film offers filmy trust to
the silent onlooker at the noisy feast,
their ghostly faces glowing with collusion; us
possessing now in fantasy
what later we displayed in mime
playing with deceit and inattention
till they become a building
and you are allowed a chair inside the building

The image of those caring people
drifted away
is stuck back together but holds no milk,
the partitioned buying intact
pictures as a consolation

The bulimic gorging of trust
waking the deeper circuits, the deep eye
soft and smooth to poison
spewing sweet liquids

## Les Paul's Garage Studio

On the dressing-table with the nail-paint,
Pfleumer's rolled gold skin that stayed
On tips of gold-lipped cigarettes
And never left a leaf of Pharaoh's smile.

Folding the sound, from the foil of scruples,
He sprayed a metal paste on plastic strip
And sold it to BASF for a
Minstrel cotton, a textile vortex.
From jeweller's wire
To suffusions of aniline dye
How small were the ripples
That laid the sand; how big were the
Blusters of musical smoke, from Ludwigshafen
And downstream.

Les Paul stripped the first Ampex that shipped
And added a fourth head
Turned, and walked straight into
Kiss of mirror halves of sound shell
Turned, and walked straight into
Brilliant cocoon from lacquer appliqué
Turned, and walked straight into
A stretch steady for four mint copies
Turned, and walked straight into
Wekausha, Wisconsin
By the river that runs both ways

By lost time that paints on loops
Aligned, looking down
From a ridge between two patterns,
Cutting silver away
To chase a picture on silver.
Butting sashes of fine shaved sound
A mask of narcissistic blond wood
With American-classic semiconductors pointing thataway

You put germanium together with Germany
That's when you've got
Purposeful distortions of the recorded groove

Linger o phantom as I retouch our mood
Flattering the
Dissipations of a simulacrum,
A dupe of time regained
A garage like that will never end

The Ampex Memphis pickup and fixit man
Says, Why that music won't stick to the tape
Because you haven't lubricated the tape

www.ingramcontent.com/pod-product-compliance
Lightning Source LLC
Chambersburg PA
CBHW031207160426
43193CB00008B/541